**Mel Bay Presents**

# 101 Three-Chord Songs
## for Guitar, Banjo, and Uke

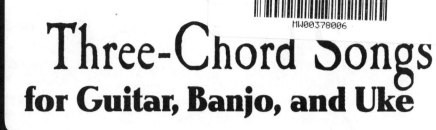

### by Larry McCabe

1 2 3 4 5 6 7 8 9 0

*Visit us on the Web at www.melbay.com — E-mail us at email@melbay.com*

# CONTENTS

# INTRODUCTION

While I was working on this book it occurred to me that maybe we should have called it *The World's Easiest Guitar Book*. But then I realized that we could have given the book many names, including *Band in a Book;* or *America's Favorite Songs;* or *Three Chords to Guitar Glory;* or even *Fun, Fun, Fun with Three Chords*. In the end, I decided that the title was not nearly as important as the songs–and the fun you and your friends are going to have strumming and singing them.

This book contains a great collection of your favorite songs in many styles: Old-time, bluegrass, gospel, Christmas, children's, cowboy, British and Celtic, seafaring, blues, and more. The great thing about the arrangements is that you can accompany every song in this book with only three chords, G, C and D7. So, if you are just starting out–or if you are a "casual player" on a chording instrument–no problem. Just learn the three chords and you will soon know enough songs to play in the parlor, on the front porch, at church, around the campfire, or at your next Friday night fish fry.

I hope that all you pickers and singers enjoy playing the songs as much as I have enjoyed arranging them. Have fun!

*Larry McCabe*
Tallahassee, Florida

# CHORDS USED IN THIS BOOK

X   Do not play this string    1   First finger (index)    3   Third finger (ring)
O   Play this string open     2   Second finger (middle)    4   Fourth finger (little)

## GUITAR CHORDS

You can play every song in this book with only three chords, G, C, and D7. Beginners can start with these chords:

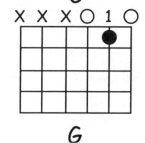

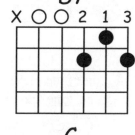

You can also play the "complete" C and G chords. Notice that there are two possible fingerings for the G chord.

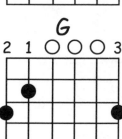

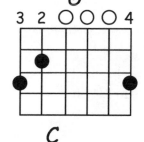

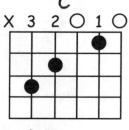

## 5-STRING BANJO CHORDS

The open fifth string can be strummed (open) with both G and C. It sounds better if the fifth string is not strummed with D7.

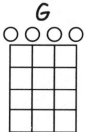

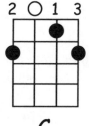

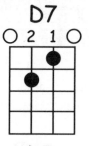

## UKELELE CHORDS

Tune the uke G-C-E-A. Tip: The first finger holds down ("barres") three strings on the D7 chord.

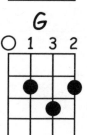

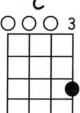

TUNING: G  C  E  A

# EASY CHORD STRUMS

• You can strum chords with either a pick or your thumb.
• Play any chord(s) you like to practice these easy strums.

4/4 means "four beats to the measure." The easiest way to play in 4/4 is to strum down four times in each measure. Use a down-pick motion ⊓ and count "<u>one</u> <u>two</u> <u>three</u> <u>four</u>," strumming a chord on each count:

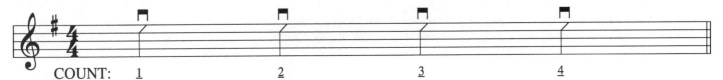

Strum two times in each measure for songs in 2/4 time:

• The simple two-beat strum can also be used in *cut time* ₵ (cut time also has two beats per measure).

3/4 time is also called "waltz time." There are three beats to the measure in 3/4 time, so strum three times, one strum on each beat. Tap your foot on each beat to help keep time:

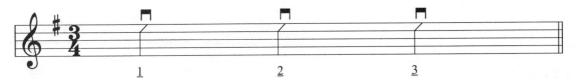

The plain *downbeat* strum can be livened up by adding *upbeat* strums. Pick the upbeat strums with an upward motion of the pick ∨ (or thumb, if you are strumming with your thumb). The following example, in 4/4 time, is counted "<u>one</u> and <u>two</u> and <u>three</u> and <u>four</u> and":

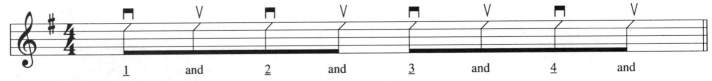

For variety, mix the "downbeat only" (quarter notes) and the "down-up" (paired eighth notes) strums, as shown in the following example in 3/4 time:

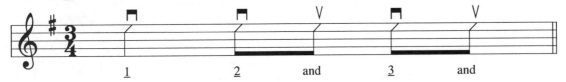

The quarter-note strums (downbeat only) and the paired eighth-note strums (down-up) can be combined in many ways. Here are a couple of nice-sounding possibilities in 4/4 time:

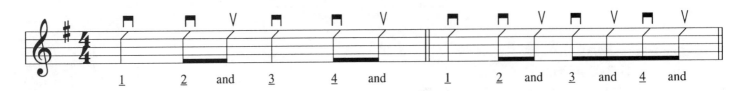

# SINGING THE SONGS

## THE STARTING NOTE

A "starting note" is given at the beginning of each song. <u>The starting note is the pitch of the first note of the song as it relates to the guitar.</u> For example, if the starting note is the "open fourth string," you can pluck that guitar string to hear the first note of the song.

A five-string banjo can also be used to find the starting note, but only for songs that start on strings 2, 3, and 4. Our "starting note" concept cannot be applied to ukeleles.

## CHANGING THE OCTAVE OR THE KEY

All the songs in this book are in the key of G. Singers will sometimes find it helpful to sing the given starting note one octave lower or higher. After deciding on the octave for the starting note, sing through several bars of the song to see if the melody "fits" your voice. All singers will find that for some songs the key of G is not their best vocal key.

If the song is difficult to sing in G, the guitarist can use a *capo* (a simple clamp, available at any music store) to change from the key of G to a more suitable vocal key. The capo can be placed at any fret, and the picker can still strum the G, C, and D7 chords, without having to learn new chord fingerings (see below).

Ukelele players can use a capo, too (use a mandolin capo if you can't find a uke capo). Banjo players can use a capo, but the fifth string must also be capoed on the five-string banjo.

## USING THE CAPO TO CHANGE KEYS

Each fret represents a half-step increase in pitch. Therefore, if the capo is placed at the first fret, and the chords are played in G, the actual key will be A-flat.

The following list shows the "actual" key when the capo is used with chords in the key of G:

First fret = Key of <u>A flat</u>

Second fret = Key of <u>A</u>

Third fret = Key of <u>B flat</u>

Fourth fret = Key of <u>B</u>

Fifth fret = Key of <u>C</u>

<u>In practice, the capo is seldom used beyond the fifth fret.</u> Nevertheless, here are some higher capo positions as they relate to the key of G:

Sixth fret = Key of <u>D flat</u>

Seventh fret = Key of <u>D</u>

Eighth fret = Key of <u>E flat</u>

Ninth fret = Key of <u>E</u>

Tenth fret = Key of <u>F</u>

Of course, another way to change keys is to transpose the melody and chords to the new key, and play the new chords instead of using the capo. The subject of transposing without using a capo is beyond the scope of this book; see a music teacher if you are not sure how to do this.

# AIN'T NO USE ME WORKIN' SO HARD

Starting note: Open second string.

Well, there ain't no use me work-in' so hard this morn-in',____ this morn-in', There ain't no use me work-in' so hard this eve-nin',____ this eve-nin'; Ain't no use me work-in' so hard, I got a gal in the boss man's yard, This morn-in',____ this eve-nin',____ right now.

Well, she brought me the eggs and she brought me the ham this mornin', this mornin',
She brought me the eggs and she brought me the ham this evenin', this evenin';
Brought me the eggs and she brought me the ham, don't bring a chicken, I don't give a hoot,
This mornin', this evenin', right now.

# ALL THE GOOD TIMES ARE PAST AND GONE

Starting note: Open second string.

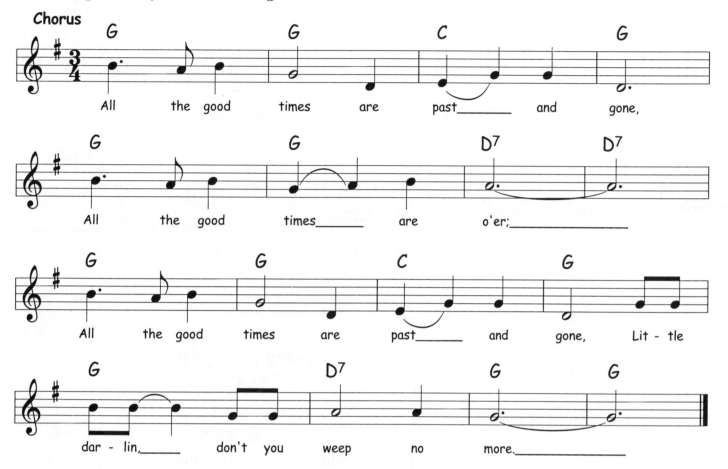

I wish to the Lord I'd never been born,
Or died when I was young;
I never would have seen your sparkling blue eyes,
Or heard your lying tongue.
*Chorus*

Now, don't you see that lonesome dove,
Flying from pine to pine;
He's mourning for his own true love
Just like I mourn for mine.
*Chorus*

Oh, can you hear that lonesome train.
A-comin' around the bend;
It's going to take me away from here,
N'er to return again.
*Chorus*

# AUNT RHODY

Starting note: Open second string.

Go tell Aunt Rho - dy, Go tell Aunt Rho - dy,

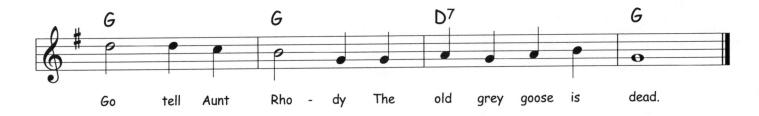

Go tell Aunt Rho - dy The old grey goose is dead.

The one she was saving,
The one she was saving,
The one she was saving
To make a feather bed.

The old gander's mourning,
The old gander's mourning,
The old gander's mourning
Because his wife is dead.

The gosling's are crying,
The gosling's are crying,
The gosling's are crying
Because their mammy's dead.

She died in the millpond,
She died in the millpond,
She died in the millpond
Her feet above her head.

# BANKS OF THE OHIO

Starting note: Open third string.

I took her by her pretty white hand,
I led her down that bank of sand;
I plunged her in where she would drown,
Lord, I saw her as she floated down.
*Chorus*

Returning home between twelve and one,
Thinking, Lord, what a deed I've done;
"I killed the girl I love, you see,
Because she would not marry me."
*Chorus*

The very next day at half past four
The sheriff walked right to my door;
He said, "Young man, don't try to run,
You'll pay for this awful crime you've done."
*Chorus*

# BARBARA ALLEN

Starting note: Open third string.

I courted her for months and years,
Thinking that I should gain her;
And oft I vowed and did declare,
No other man should have her.

I sent a man to yonder town,
To ask for Barbara Allen;
"You must come to my master's house,
If you be Barbara Allen."

So slowly she put on her clothes,
So slowly she came to him;
And when she came to his bedside,
"Young man," she said, "You're dying."

He turned his face unto the wall
And death came slowly to him;
"Adieu, adieu to all my friends,
Farewell to Barbara Allen."

And as she walked across the field
And heard his death bell tolling;
And every toll, it seemed to say,
"Hard hearted Barbara Allen."

"Oh, mother dear, make me my bed,
And make it for my sorrow;
My true love died for me today,
I'll die for him tomorrow."

So he did die on one good day,
And she died on the morrow;
And out of him sprang roses red.
And out of her a briar.

It grew and grew so very high,
Till it could grow no higher;
And around the top growed a true lover's knot,
And around it twined the briar.

# BETTY AND DUPREE

Starting note: Open fourth string.

Bet-ty told Du-pree: "I want a dia-mond ring."_____

Bet-ty told Du-pree: "I want a dia-mond ring."_____ Du-pree said:

"Oh, yes, Bet-ty, for you I'd do most an-y-thing."_____

Dupree said: "Go to sleep,
See what tomorrow brings." (2x)
"Sure as the sun comes up,
You'll get a diamond ring."

Now, Dupree he had a gun,
It was a forty-four. (2x)
He stuck it in his pocket;
Went to the jewelry store.

When Dupree went to town
With his forty-four in his hand. (2x)
He went after jewelry,
But he got the jewelry man.

Dupree hired a taxi,
Went to Memphis, Tennessee. (2x)
Dupree asked the taxi driver,
"Wonder will they hang poor me?"

Then he went to Motor City,
And he was no scary man. (2x)
He had a Colt in his pocket
And a forty-four in his hand.

Then he shot a big policeman, Lord,
And wounded sev'ral more. (2x)
One fell to his knees cryin',
"Please don't shoot me no more."

Then he went to the post office
To get his evening mail. (2x)
But they caught poor Dupree, Lord,
And sent him to Atlanta jail.

They led him to the scaffold
With a black cap over his face. (2x)
And now some lonesome graveyard
Is Dupree's restin' place.

The chorus walked behind him singin'
"Nearer My God to Thee." (2x)
Poor Betty she was cryin',
"Have mercy on Dupree."

"Sail on, sail on,
Sail on, Dupree, sail on." (2x)
"Don't mind you sailin',
But you'll be gone so dog-gone long."

# BIG BALL IN NASHVILLE

Starting note: Open third string.

**Chorus**

Big ball in Nash - ville, big ball in town;

Big ball in Nash - ville, we'll dance a - round.

Let's have a party, let's have a time;
Let's have a party, I won't need a dime.
*Chorus*

Roll on the ground, boys, roll on the ground;
Eat salty crackers, ten cents a pound.
*Chorus*

My love's in jail. boys, my love's in jail;
My love's in jail, boys, who'll go her bail?
*Chorus*

# BILLY BARLOW

Starting note: Open third string.

"What shall I hunt?" says Risky Rob,
"What shall I hunt?" says Robin to Bob;
"What shall I hunt?" says Dan'l to Joe,
"Hunt for a rat," says Billy Barlow.

"How shall I get him?" says Risky Rob,
"How shall I get him?" says Robin to Bob;
"How shall I get him?" says Dan'l to Joe,
"Go borrow a gun," says Billy Barlow.

"How shall I haul him?" says Risky Rob,
"How shall I haul him?" says Robin to Bob;
"How shall I haul him?" says Dan'l to Joe,
"Go borrow a cart," says Billy Barlow.

"How shall we divide him?" says Risky Rob,
"How shall we divide him?" says Robin to Bob;
"How shall we divide him?" says Dan'l to Joe,
"How shall we divide him?" says Billy Barlow.

"Ill take shoulder," says Risky Rob,
"I'll take side," says Robin to Bob;
"I'll take ham," says Dan'l to Joe,
"Tail bone mine," says Billy Barlow.

"How shall we cook him?" says Risky Rob,
"How shall we cook him?" says Robin to Bob;
"How shall we cook him?" says Dan'l to Joe,
"Each as you like it," says Billy Barlow.

"I'll broil shoulder," says Risky Rob,
"I'll fry side," says Robin to Bob;
"I'll boil ham," says Dan'l to Joe,
"Tail bone raw," says Billy Barlow.

# BILLY BOY

Starting note: Open second string.

Oh,____ where have you been, Bil - ly Boy, Bil - ly Boy? Oh,____ where have you been, charm - ing Bil - ly?_____ I have been to seek a wife, she's the joy____ of my life; She's a young thing and can - not leave her moth - er._____

Did she ask you to come in, Billy Boy, Billy Boy?
Did she ask you to come in, charming Billy?
Yes, she asked me to come in,
There's a dimple on her chin;
She's a young thing and cannot leave her mother.

Did she set for you a chair, Billy Boy, Billy Boy?
Did she set for you a chair, charming Billy?
Yes, she set for me a chair,
She has ringlets in her hair;
She's a young thing and cannot leave her mother.

Can she bake a cherry pie, Billy Boy, Billy Boy?
Can she bake a cherry pie, darling Billy?
She can bake a cherry pie,
Quick's a cat can wink an eye;
She's a young thing and cannot leave her mother.

# BLEST BE THE TIE THAT BINDS

Words by John Fawcett
Music by Johann G. Nageli

Starting note: Open second string.

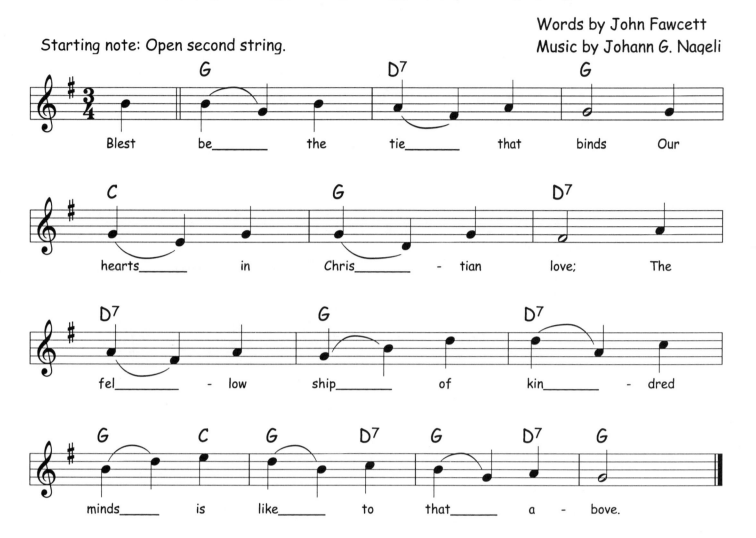

Before our father's throne we pour our ardent prayers;
Our fears, our hopes, our aims are one, our comforts and our cares.

We share our mutual woes, our mutual burdens bear;
And often for each other flows the sympathizing tear.

When we asunder part, it gives us inward pain;
But we shall still be joined in heart, and hope to meet again.

# BLOW THE MAN DOWN

Starting note: Open third string.

*Blow* means to strike or knock.

I'm a deep water sailor just in from Hong Kong,
Way, aye, blow the man down!
If you'll give me some whiskey I'll sing you my song,
Give me some time to blow the man down.

'Twas on a Black Baller I first seved my time,
Way, aye, blow the man down!
And on that Black Baller I wasted my prime,
Give me some time to blow the man down.

Pay attention to orders, now you one and all,
Way, aye, blow the man down!
But don't waste your life on the clipper Black Ball,
Give me some time to blow the man down.

# BOIL 'EM CABBAGE DOWN

Starting note: Open second string.

**Chorus**

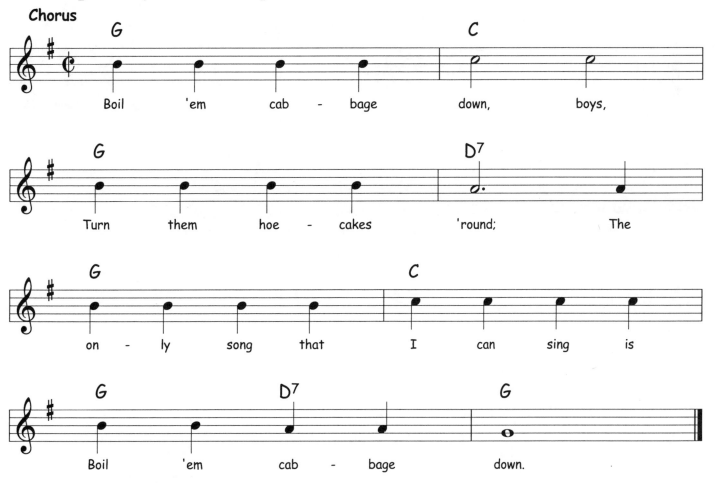

Boil 'em cab - bage down, boys,
Turn them hoe - cakes 'round; The
on - ly song that I can sing is
Boil 'em cab - bage down.

Raccoon in the 'simmon tree, possom on the ground;
Possom said to the raccoon, hey, shake some 'simmons down.
*Chorus*

Yankees come to Tennessee to steal a mule or two;
Rebel army pushed 'em back, what's old Abe gwine to do?
*Chorus*

Took my gal to the blacksmith shop to have her mouth made small;
She turned 'round a time or two, and swallowed shop and all.
*Chorus*

Granny apple in the tree, cabbage on the ground;
Grandpa had a sip of corn and run old Grandma down.
*Chorus*

Grandpa had a muley cow, muley since it's born;
It took a jaybird forty years to fly from horn to horn.
*Chorus*

# BURY ME BENEATH THE WILLOW

Starting note: Third fret, second string.

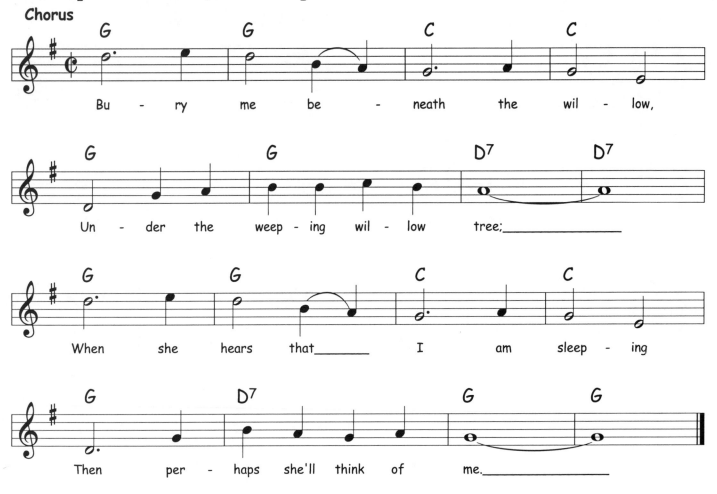

**Chorus**

Bu - ry me be - neath the wil - low,

Un - der the weep - ing wil - low tree;_____

When she hears that_____ I am sleep - ing

Then per - haps she'll think of me._____

My heart is sad and I'm in sorrow,
For the only one I love;
When shall I see her? Oh, no never,
'Til we meet in heav'n above.
*Chorus*

Tomorrow was to be our wedding,
Lord, oh Lord, where can she be?
She's gone, she's gone to love another;
And she cares no more for me.
*Chorus*

She told me that she did not love me,
How could I know it was true?
Until an angel softly whispered,
She is proving untrue to you.
*Chorus*

Bury me 'neath the weeping willow
In the meadow where we met;
To show the world that I died grieving
For a love I can't forget.
*Chorus*

# CAMPTOWN RACES

Starting note: Third fret, second string.

Stephen Foster

Camp - town la - dies sing this song, Doo - dah!
Come down here with my hat caved in, Doo - dah!

doo - dah! Camp - town race - track five miles long,
doo - dah! Go back home with a pock - et full of tin,

**Chorus**

Oh! doo - dah day! Gwine to run all night!
Oh! doo - dah day!

Gwine to run all day! I'll bet my mon - ey on a

bob - tail nag, Some - bod - y bet on the bay.

The long-tail filly and the big black hoss, Doo-dah! doo-dah!
They fly the track and they both cut across, Oh! doo-dah day!
The blind hoss sticken' in a big mud hole, Doo-dah! doo-dah!
Can't touch bottom with a ten-foot pole, Oh! doo-dah day!
*Chorus*

Old muley cow come on to the track, Doo-dah! doo-dah!
The bobtail fling her over his back, Oh! doo-dah day!
Then fly along like a railroad car, Doo-dah! doo-dah!
Runnin' a race with a shootin' star, Oh! doo-dah day!
*Chorus*

# CARELESS LOVE

Starting note: Open second string.

Love, oh love, oh care - less love,_____

Love, oh love, oh care - less love;_____

Love, oh love, oh care - less love, You

see what care - less love has done.

I cried last night and the night before, (3x)
Gonna cry tonight, then cry no more.

Sorrow, sorrow, to my heart, (3x)
When me and my true love have to part.

Love, oh love, oh careless love,
You fly to my head like wine;
You've wrecked the life of many a poor gal,
And you nearly took this life of mine.

It's gone and broke this heart of mine, (3x)
And it'll break that heart of yours sometime.

I love my mama and papa, too, (3x)
But I'd leave them both and go with you.

Love, oh love, oh careless love,
In your clutches of desire;
You made me break a many true vow,
Then you set my very soul on fire.

# COME AND GO WITH ME

Starting note: Open fourth string.

There ain't no bowing in that land,
Ain't no bowing in that land,
Ain't no bowing in that land where I'm bound;
There ain't no bowing in that land,
Ain't no bowing in that land,
Ain't no bowing in that land where I'm bound.

There ain't no kneeling in that land . . .

There's peace and freedom in that land . . .

# CORINNE, CORINNA

Starting note: Second fret, fifth string.

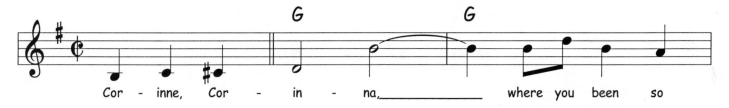

Cor - inne, Cor - in - na,_____ where you been so

long?_____ Cor - inne, Cor - in - na,_____

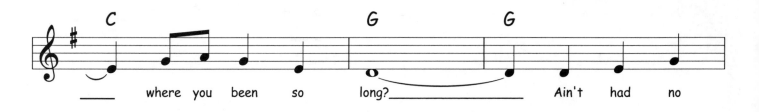

_____ where you been so long?_____ Ain't had no

lov - in'_____ since you been gone._____

Corinne, Corinna, where'd you stay last night? (2x)
Come home this morning, sun was shining bright.

I love Corinna, tell the world I do. (2x)
Just a little more lovin'; make your heart beat true.

Corinne, Corinna, its-a fare you well (2).
Where I might be goin' no one can tell.

# COTTON-EYED JOE

Starting note: Open second string.

Get down the fid - dle and ros - in up the bow,

Play a lit - tle tune called cot - ton eyed Joe.

**Chorus**

Where did you come from, where did you go?

Where did you come from, Cot - ton Eyed Joe?

Where did you come from, where did you go?

Where did you come from, Cot - ton Eyed Joe?

Cornstalk fiddle
And a cornstalk bow:
Cotton-Eyed Joe
Doin' a jig on the floor.
*Chorus*

Gonna load up
My old forty-four;
Shoot a couple possums
For the folks comin' o'er.
*Chorus*

Jumped out of bed
And stumped my toe;
Call the doctor,
Cotton-Eyed Joe.
*Chorus*

# THE CRAWDAD SONG

Starting note: Open third string.

Get up old man, you slept too late, honey,
Get up old man, you slept too late, babe;
Get up old man, you slept too late,
The crawdad man done passed your gate,
Honey, sugar baby, mine.

What'cha gonna do when the lake runs dry, honey,
What'cha gonna do when the lake runs dry, babe;
What'cha gonna do when the lake runs dry,
Sit on the bank and watch the crawdads die,
Honey, sugar baby, mine.

Sal's old pappy's got a mean streak, honey,
Sal's old pappy's got a mean streak, babe;
Sal's old pappy's got a mean streak,
'Lows her out crawdaddin' one time a week,
Honey, sugar baby, mine.

# DARK HOLLOW

Starting note: Open second string.

So blow your whistle freight train,
Blow it far on down the track;
I'm goin' away, I'm leavin' today,
I'm goin' but I ain't comin' back.

I'd rather be in some dark hollow,
Where the sun refused to shine;
Than to be stuck in some big city,
In a motel with you on my mind.

This song actually has four chords, but the author feels compelled to include it in the book, anyway.

# DIXIE

Starting note: Open second string.

Dan Emmett

Oh, I wish I was in the land of cot-ton, Old times there are
In Dix-ie land where I was born in, Ear-ly on one

not for-got-ten; Look a-way, look a-way, look a-
fros-ty mor-nin'; Look a-way, look a-way, look a-

way, Dix-ie land. I wish I was in
way, Dix-ie land.

Dix-ie, a-way, a-way, In Dix-ie land I'll

take my stand to live and die in Dix-ie; A-

way, a-way, a-way down South in Dix-ie, A-

way, a-way, a-way down South in Dix-ie.

There's buckwheat cakes and Injun batter,
Makes you fat or a little fatter;
Look away, look away, look away, Dixie land.
Then hoe it down and scratch your gravel,
To Dixie's Land I'm bound to travel,
Look away, look away, look away, Dixie land.
*Chorus*

28

# DOWN IN THE VALLEY

Starting note: Open fourth string.

Down in the val - ley,_____ The

Val - ley so low;_____

Hang your head o - ver,_____

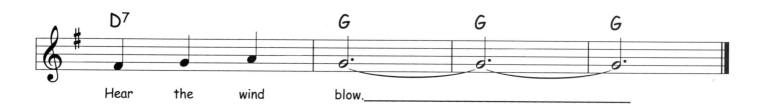

Hear the wind blow._____

Hear the wind blow, dear,
Hear the wind blow;
Hang your head over,
Hear the wind blow.

Roses love sunshine,
Violets love dew;
Angels in heaven,
Know I love you.

Know I love you, dear,
Know I love you;
Angels in heaven,
Know I love you.

29

# EARLY ONE MORNING

Starting note: Open third string.

Ear - ly one morn - ing, just as the sun was ris - ing, I

heard a maid - en sing___ in the val - ley be - low.

**Refrain**

"Oh, don't de - ceive___ me, Oh, nev - er leave___ me,

How___ could you use___ a___ poor___ mai - den so?"

"Remember the vows that you made to me truly,
Remember the day that you vowed to be true."
*Refrain*

"Gay are the garlands and red are the roses,
I picked from the garden to bind on my brow."
*Refrain*

Thus sang the maiden, her sorrow bewailing,
Thus sang the poor maid in the valley below.
*Refrain*

# EAST VIRGINIA BLUES

Starting note: Open second string.

I was born_____ in East Vir - gin - ia,_____ North Car - o -

li_____ - na I did go;_____ There I

met_____ the fair - est maid - en,_____ Whose name and

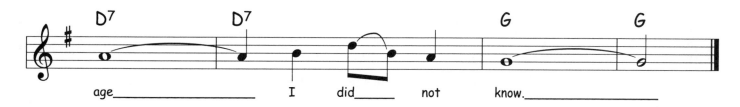

age_____ I did_____ not know._____

Well, her hair was dark in color,
And here cheeks were rosy red;
On her breast she wore white lilies,
Where I longed to lay my head.

Papa says we cannot marry,
Mama says you'll never do;
If you ever learn to love me
I will run away with you.

I'd rather be in some dark holler,
Where the sun refused to shine;
Than to see you with another,
And to know you can't be mine.

I don't want your greenback dollars,
I don't want your watch and chain;
All I want is your love, darling,
Say that you will be mine again.

When I sleep I'm dreaming of you,
When I'm awake I have no rest;
Minutes seem to me like hours
With aches and pains all through my head.

In my heart you are my darling,
At my door you're welcome in;
By my gate I'll always greet you,
Say you'll let your love come in.

# FAIR ELEANOR

Starting note: Open fourth string.

"Fath - er, oh, fath - er, come rid - dle to me, Come, rid - dle it all_____ as one; And tell me wheth - er to mar - ry fair El - len, Or bring the Brown girl home."_____

"The Brown girl has houses and land,
Fair Eleanor she has none;
Wherefore I charge you upon my blessing
"To bring the Brown girl home."

Away he rode to Eleanor's house,
And knocked upon her door;
No one was so ready as fair Eleanor
To greet Lord Thomas once more.

"What news, what news, what news? she cried,
What news hast thou brought unto me?"
"I am come to bid the to my wedding,
Beneath the sycamore tree."

"Heaven forbid that any such thing
Should ever pass by my side;
I thought that thou wouldst have been my
husband
And I would be your bride."

"Oh, mother, oh mother, would you go or stay?"
"Fair child, I beg you not go.
For I'm afraid you'll never return
To see your dear mother any more."

Eleanor dressed in her satin so fine,
Her sisters dressed in green;
And ev'ry town that she rode through
They took her for a queen.

She rode till she came to Lord Thomas's house,
She tingled so loud at the ring;
And no one so ready as Thomas himself
To let fair Eleanor in.

He took her by her lily-white hand,
And led her through the hall;
And sat her down in the noblest chair
Amongst the ladies all.

The Brown girl had a little penknife,
It's blade was both long and sharp;
Between the long ribs and the short
She pierced Fair Eleanor's heart.

Lord Thomas he had a sword by his side,
As he walked through the hall;
He took off the Brown girl's head from her
shoulders
And flung it against the wall.

He put the handle to the ground,
The sword unto his heart;
No sooner did three lovers meet,
No sooner did they part.

"Father, oh father, go dig my grave,
Go dig it wide and deep;
And lay fair Eleanor by my side,
And the Brown girl at my feet."

# FOGGY MOUNTAIN TOP

Starting note: Open second string.

**Chorus**

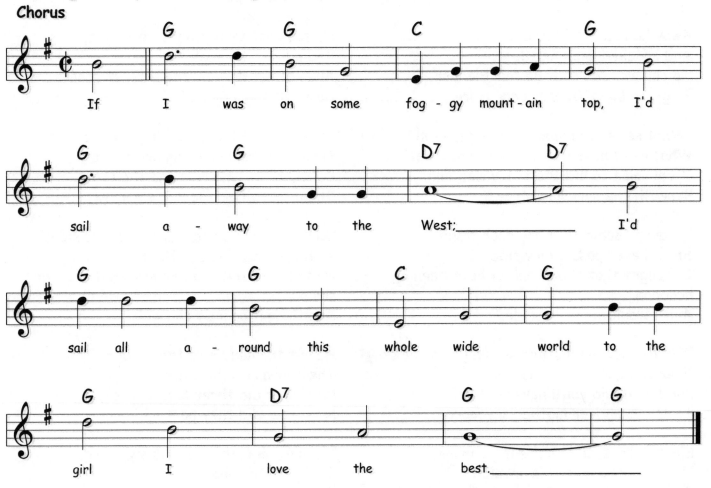

If I was on some fog-gy mount-ain top, I'd
sail a-way to the West;_____ I'd
sail all a-round this whole wide world to the
girl I love the best._____

If I'd have listened to what mama said
I would not be in here today;
A-lyin' around this old jailhouse
Just wasting my poor life away.
*Chorus*

Oh, she caused me to weep, she caused me to mourn,
She caused me to leave my home;
Oh the lonesome pines and the good old times,
I'm on my way back home.
*Chorus*

# FRANKIE AND JOHNNY

Also known as "Frankie and Albert."

Starting note: Open third string.

Frankie was a good woman,
Everybody knows,
She spent a hundred dollars
For to buy her man some clothes,
He was her man,
But he was doin' her wrong.

Frankie went down to the barroom,
Asked for a glass of beer,
Said to Joe, the bartender:
"Has my lovin' Johnny been here?"
He was her man,
But he was doin' her wrong.

Well, when Frankie shot Johnny,
He fell down on his knees,
Looked at Frankie and told her:
"Don't shoot me no mo', please."
He was her man,
But he's dead and gone.

Frankie followed Johnny to the graveyard,
Fell down upon her knees,
"Please say some words to me, Johnny,
And give my heart some peace,
You was my man,
But you was doin' me wrong."

Frankie said to the sheriff,
"What will the old judge do?"
"Strap you in the 'lectric chair,
And send thirty thousand volts through you.
Johnny was your man,
But you gunned him down."

Hearse took her to the graveyard,
They put her into the ground,
Now all that's left of Frankie is
A wooden cross and a mound.
He was her man,
And now they're both dead and gone.

# GOODBYE, OLD PAINT

Starting note: Second fret, fourth string.

I'm a-ridin' Old Paint,
I'm a-leadin' Old Dan;
Good mornin', little Annie,
I'm off for Montan'.
*Chorus*

Oh, hitch up your horses,
And feed them some hay;
And seat yourself by me
As long as you stay.
*Chorus*

My horses ain't hungry,
They'll not eat your hay;
My wagon is loaded
And rolling away.
*Chorus*

# GREEN GROW THE LILACS

Starting note: Open fourth string.

I used to have a sweetheart, but now I have none,
Since she's gone and left me, I care not for one;
Since she's gone and left me, contented I'll be,
For she loves another one better than me.

I passed my love's window, both early and late,
The look that she gave me, it made my heart ache;
Oh, the look that she gave me was painful to see,
For she loves another one better than me.

I wrote my love letters in rosy red lines,
She sent me an answer all twisted in twines;
Saying, "Keep your love letters and don't waste your time,
Just you write to your love and I'll write to mine."

# GYPSY DAVY

Starting note: Open third string.

I was a high - born gen - tle - man,

She was a high - born la - dy; We

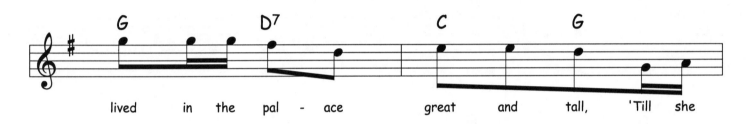

lived in the pal - ace great and tall, 'Till she

met with Gyp - sy Da - vy.

She smiled to leave her husband dear
And go with the Gypsy Davy;
But the tears came trickling down her cheeks
When she thought of her blue-eyed baby.

Have you forsaken your house and home,
Have you forsaken your baby?
Have you forsaken your husband dear
To go with Gypsy Davy?

He saddled up his buckskin horse
And a hundred-dollar saddle;
"Point out to me their wagon tracks
And after them I'll travel."

Last night she slept in a feather bed,
With her arms around her baby;
Tonight she lies in the cold, cold ground
In the arms of her Gypsy Davy.

# HAND ME DOWN MY WALKING CANE

Starting note: Open fourth string.

I got high_____ and I got in jail,_____ Lord, I got
high_____ and I got in jail;_____ I got
high and I got in jail, I had no - bo - dy for to go my bail, My
sins they have o - ver - tak - en me._____

Hand me down my bottle of corn,
Oh, hand me down my bottle of corn;
Hand me down my bottle of corn,
Gonna get drunk as sure as you're born,
My sins they have overtaken me.

Oh, the beans was tough and the meat was fat,
The beans was tough and the meat was fat;
Oh, the beans was tough and the meat was fat,
Oh, good God, I couldn't eat that,
My sins they have overtaken me.

Lordy if I die in Tennessee,
Lordy, if I die in Tennessee;
If I die in Tennessee
Ship me back by C.O.D.,
My sins they have overtaken me.

Hand me down my walking cane,
Oh, hand me down my walking cane;
Hand me down my walking cane,
Gonna by gone on the midnight train,
My sins they have overtaken me.

# HANDSOME MOLLY

Starting note: Open fourth string.

I wish I were in Lon - don, or

some oth - er sea - port town; I'd set my foot on a

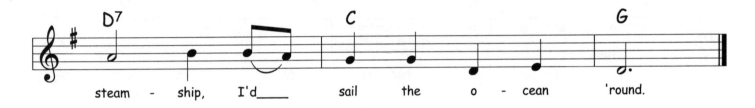

steam - ship, I'd____ sail the o - cean 'round.

While sailing 'round the ocean,
While sailing 'round the sea;
I'll think of handsome Molly
Wherever she may be.

I'll go down to the river
When everyone's asleep;
I'll think of handsome Molly
And then lay down and weep.

You rode to church last Sunday,
You looked and passed me by;
I know your mind is changin'
By the rovin' of your eye.

Don't you remember, Molly,
You gave me your right hand?
You said if ever you married
That I would be your man.

# HE'S GOT THE WHOLE WORLD IN HIS HANDS

Starting note: Third fret, second string.

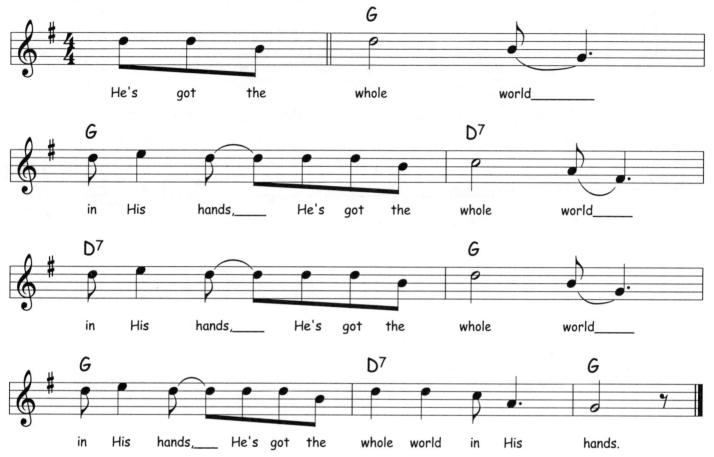

He's got the little bitty babies in His hands, (3x)
He's got the whole world in His hands.

He's got you and me, brother, in His hands, (3x)
He's got the whole world in His hands.

He's got the liars and the gamblers in His hands, (3x)
He's got the whole world in His hands.

He's got the television preachers in His hands, (3x)
He's got the whole world in His hands.

He's got the honky-tonk hustlers in His hands, (3x)
He's got the whole world in His hands.

He's got the crooked politicians in His hands, (3x)
He's got the whole world in His hands.

# HOME SWEET HOME

Words by John Howard Payne
Music by Henry Bishop

Starting note: Open third string.

An exile from home, splendor dazzles in vain,
Oh, give me my lowly thatched cottage again;
The birds singing gaily, that come at my call,
Give me them, with that peace of mind, dearer than all.
Chorus

To thee, I'll return, overburdened with care,
The heart's dearest solace will smile on me there;
No more from that cottage again will I roam,
Be it ever so humble, there's no place like home.
Chorus

# HOUSE OF THE RISING SUN
## (RISING SUN BLUES)

*Slow shuffle blues*

Starting note: Third fret, second string.

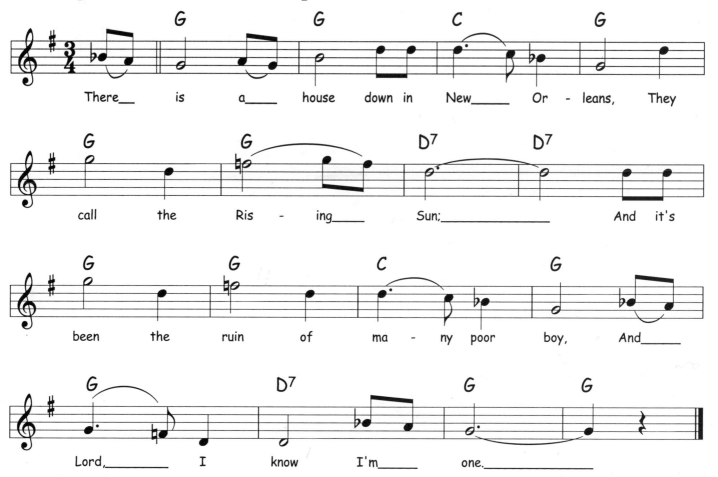

Go fill your glasses to the brim,
Let the drinks flow merrily around;
And we'll drink to the health of a ramblin' boy
Who roamed from town to town.

The only thing that a gambler needs
Is his suitcase and a trunk;
And the only time he's satisfied
Is when he's all a-drunk.

Please tell my youngest brother
Not to do what I have done;
But to shun that house in New Orleans
They call the Rising Sun.

Now, boys, don't believe what a girl tells you,
Though her eyes be blue or brown;
Unless she's on some scaffold high
Saying, "Boys, I can't come down."

I'm goin' back to New Orleans,
For my race is nearly run;
Gonna spend the rest of my wicked life
Beneath that Rising Sun.

# HOW MANY BISCUITS CAN YOU EAT?

Starting note: Open third string.

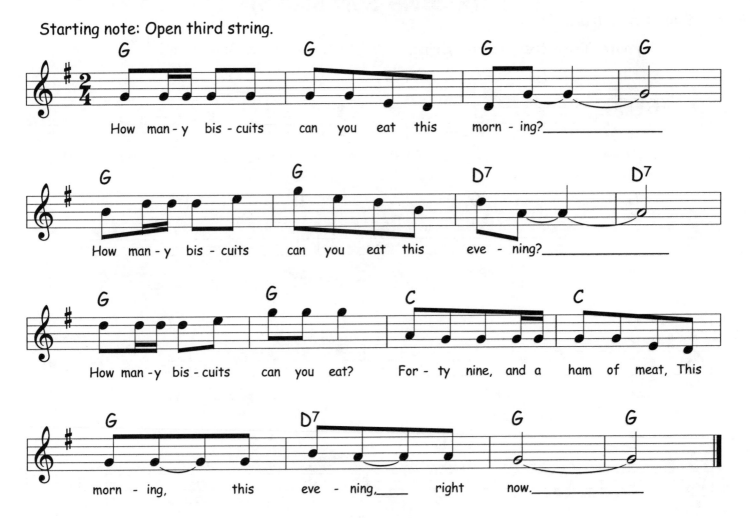

Performance note: Some performers stop playing in measures 11-12, and the lyrics are spoken.

Well, when you see me looking straight this morning,
When you see me looking straight this evening;
When you see me looking straight, you'll see me lookin' at that biscuit plate,
This morning, this evening, right now.

Well, wake up Sally, you slept too late this morning,
Wake up Sally, you slept to late this evening;
Wake up Sally, you slept too late, there ain't another biscuit on that plate,
This morning, this evening, right now.

She killed that chicken and saved me the head this morning
She killed that chicken and saved me the head this evening;
She killed that chicken and she saved me the head,
She thought I was a-workin', but I was lyin' in bed,
This morning, this evening, right now.

# HUSH, LITTLE BABY

Starting note: Open fourth string.

Hush, lit - tle ba - by don't say a word,

Pa - pa's gon - na buy you a mock - ing bird; And

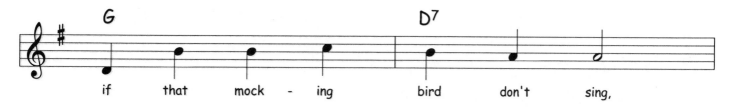

if that mock - ing bird don't sing,

Pa - pa's gon - na buy you a dia - mond ring.

And if that diamond ring turns brass,
Papa's gonna buy you a looking glass;
And if that looking glass is broke,
Papa's gonna buy you a billy goat.

And if that billy goat don't pull,
Papa's gonna buy you a cart and bull;
And if that cart and bull turn over,
Papa's gonna buy you a dog named Rover.

And if that dog named Rover won't bark,
Papa's gonna buy you a horse and cart;
And if that horse and cart fall down,
You're still the sweetest little baby in town.

# I AM A PILGRIM

Starting note: Open fourth string.

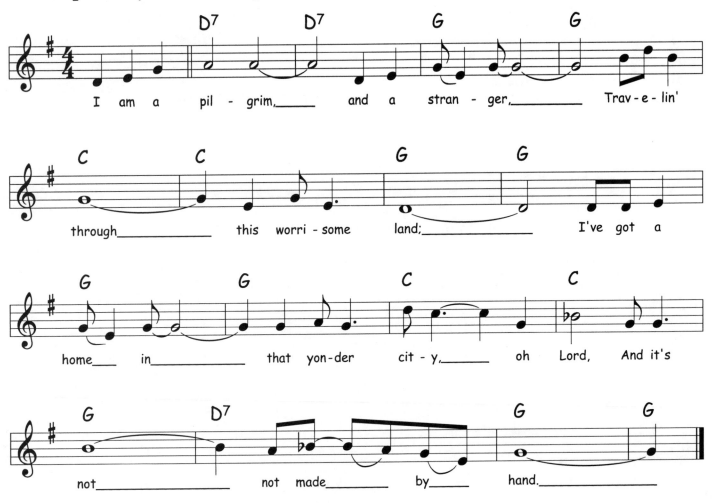

I've got a mother, a sister and a brother,
Who have gone to that sweet land;
I'm determined to go and see them, good Lord,
All over on that distant shore.

As I go down to that river of Jordan,
Just to bathe my weary soul;
If I could touch but the hem of His garment, good Lord,
Well, I believe it would make me whole.

# I NEVER WILL MARRY

Starting note: Open third string.

"I nev - er will mar - ry,_____ I will
be no man's wife;_____ I ex -
pect to be sin - gle,_____ All the
rest of my life."_____

| One day as I rambled | "My love's gone and left me, |
|---|---|
| Down by the seashore; | He's the one I adore; |
| The wind it did whistle | He's gone where I never |
| And the waters did roar. | Shall see him no more." |
| | |
| I heard a fair maiden | "The shells in the ocean |
| Make a pitiful cry; | Will be my death bed; |
| She sounded so lonesome | The fish in deep water |
| By the waters nearby. | Swim over my head." |

She plunged her fair body
In the waters so deep;
She closed her big blue eyes
Forever to sleep.

# IN THE SWEET BYE AND BYE

Words by S. Fillmore Bennett
Music by J.P. Webster

Starting note: Open third string.

We shall sing on that beautiful shore,
The melodious songs of the blest;
And our spirits shall sorrow no more,
Not a sigh for the blessing of rest.
*Chorus*

To our bountiful Father above,
We will offer the tribute of praise;
For the glorious gift of his love,
And the blessings that hallow our days.
*Chorus*

*Photo by Larry McCabe*

# I SAW THREE SHIPS

And what was in those ships all three,
On Christmas Day, on Christmas Day;
And what was in those ships all three,
On Christmas Day in the morning.

The Virgin Mary and Christ were there,
On Christmas Day, on Christmas Day;
The Virgin Mary and Christ were there,
On Christmas Day in the morning.

# IT AIN'T GONNA RAIN NO MORE

Starting note: Open fourth string.

It ain't gon - na rain no more, no more, It

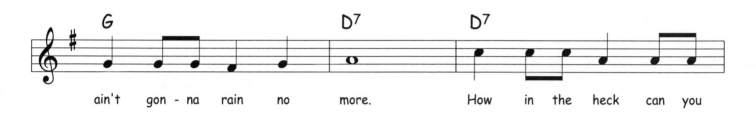

ain't gon - na rain no more. How in the heck can you

scrub your neck if it ain't going to rain no more?

It ain't gonna rain, it ain't gonna snow,
It ain't gonna rain no more;
Ain't gonna thunder and ain't gonna pour,
Ain't gonna rain no more.

Oh, what did the blackbird say to the crow?
It ain't gonna rain no more;
Ain't gonna hail, ain't gonna snow,
Ain't gonna rain no more.

Bake them biscuits good and brown,
It ain't gonna rain no more;
Swing your ladies 'round and 'round,
Ain't gonna rain no more.

# I WISH I WAS SINGLE AGAIN

Starting note: Open fourth string.

**Chorus**

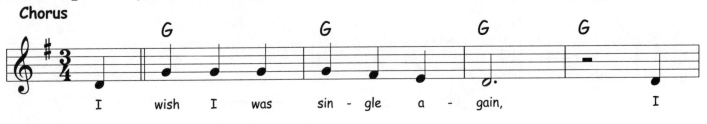

I wish I was sin - gle a - gain, I

wish I was sin - gle a - gain; For

if I was sin - gle my pock - ets would jin - gle, I

wish I was sin - gle a - gain.

I married a wife, O then,
I married a wife, O then;
I married a wife,
She's the plague of my life,
And I wish I was single again.
*Chorus*

My wife she died, O then,
My wife she died, O then;
My wife she died,
I laughed 'till I cried,
To think I was single again.
*Chorus*

I married another, O then,
I married another, O then;
I married another,
The devil's grandmother,
I wish I was single again.
*Chorus*

She beat me, she banged me, O then,
She beat me, she banged me, O then;
She beat me, she banged me,
She swore she would hang me,
I wish I was single again.
*Chorus*

# JACOB'S LADDER

Starting note: Open second string.

Every round goes higher, higher, (3 times)
Soldiers of the cross.

Every rung goes higher, higher, (3 times)
Soldiers of the cross.

Sinner, do you love my Jesus? (3 times)
Soldiers of the cross.

If you love Him, why not serve Him? (3 times)
Soldiers of the cross.

We are climbing higher, higher, (3 times)
Soldiers of the cross.

Rise, shine, give God glory, (3 times)
Soldiers of the cross.

# JESSE JAMES

Starting note: Open fourth string.

Jes - se James was a lad who killed ma - ny a man, He robbed the Glen - dale train;_____ He took from the rich and gave to the poor, He'd a heart and a hand and a brain._____ Oh,

**Chorus**

Jes - se had a wife who mourned for his life, Three chil - dren, they were brave;_____ But that dir - ty lit - tle cow - ard who shot Mis - ter How - ard Has laid poor Jes - se in his grave._____

It was on a Wednesday night, the moon was shining bright,
They robbed the Glendale train;
The people they did say, for many miles away,
It was robbed by Frank and Jesse James.
*Chorus*

The people held their breath when they heard of Jesse's death,
And wondered how he ever came to die;
It was one of the gang called little Robert Ford,
He shot poor Jesse on the sly.
*Chorus*

It was Robert Ford, that dirty little coward,
I wonder how he does feel;
For he ate of Jesse's bread and he slept in Jesse's bed,
And he laid poor Jesse in his grave.
*Chorus*

It was on a Saturday night, Jesse was at home,
Talking with his family brave;
Robert Ford came along like a thief in the night
And laid poor Jesse in his grave.
*Chorus*

Jesse went to his rest with his hand upon his breast,
The devil may be upon his knee;
He was born one day in the county of Clay
And came from a solitary race.
*Chorus*

This song was made by Billy Gashade,
As soon as the news did arrive;
He said there was no man with the law in his hand,
Who could take Jesse James when alive.
*Chorus*

# JESUS LOVES ME

Starting note: Third fret, second string.

Je - sus loves me this I know, For the Bi - ble tells me so;

Lit - tle ones to Him be - long, They are weak but He is strong.

**Chorus**

Yes, Je - sus loves me! Yes, Je - sus loves me!

Yes, Je - sus loves me! The Bi - ble tells me so.

Jesus loves me He who died, heaven's gate to open wide;
He will wash away my sins, let His little child come in.
*Chorus*

Jesus loves me He will stay close beside me all the way;
If I love Him when I die, He will take me home on high.
*Chorus*

# JIM ALONG JOSIE

Starting note: Third fret, second string.

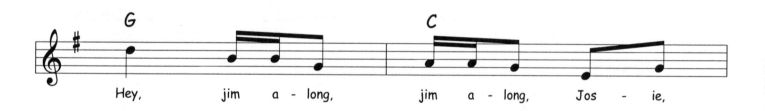

Walk, jim along, jim along, Josie,
Walk, jim along, jim along, Jo;
Walk, jim along, jim along, Josie,
Walk, jim along, jim along, Jo.

Hop . . .

Crawl . . .

Skip . . .

Jump . . .

Run . . .

Performance tips:

1) Vary the speed-and the accenting of key words-according to the specific lyric. For example, sing "hop" with a "bouncy" feel, play slow on "crawl," and so on.

2) The first verse "Hey, jim along . . ." can be used as a chorus, if you wish.

# JINGLE BELLS

Starting note: Open second string.

James Pierpont

# JOE TURNER BLUES

Starting note: Third fret, second string.

W.C. Handy

Sweet babe, I'm gonna leave you, and the time ain't long; (2x)
If you don't believe I'm leavin', just count the days I'm gone.

I bought a bulldog to watch you while you sleep; (2x)
And now you got the nerve to call Joe Turner "cheap."

You make me feel like nothin', somethin' throwed away; (2x)
Gonna pick my guitar, play the blues all day.

# JOHN HENRY

Starting note: Third fret, second string.

John___ Hen - ry was a lit - tle ba - by boy You could
hold him in the palm of your hand; The___ last words that his
dad - dy ev - er said, Said, "You're gon - na be a steel___ driv - in'
man, Lord, Lord, Yes, you're gon - na be a steel___ driv - in' man."

John Henry told his captain,
That a man was a natural man;
An before he'd let that steam drill beat him down,
He'd die with his hammer in his hand, Lord, Lord,
He'd die with his hammer in his hand.

Captain said to John Henry:
"Gonna bring that steam drill 'round;
Take that steel drill out on the job,
Gonna whoop that steel on down, Lord, Lord,
Gonna whoop that steel on down."

John Henry went down to the railroad
With a twelve-pound hammer by his side;
He walked down the track but he didn't come back,
'Cause he laid down his hammer and he died, Lord, Lord,
Yes, he laid down his hammer and he died.

John Henry hammered in the mountains,
The mountains was so high;
The last words I heard the poor boy say:
"Gimme a drink of water 'fore I die, Lord, Lord,
Gimme a cool drink of water 'fore I die."

John Henry had a pretty little gal,
And her name was Polly Ann;
John Henry took sick and he had to go to bed,
Polly drove steel like a man, Lord, Lord,
Polly drove with her hammer like a man.

John Henry had another woman,
The dress she wore was red;
The last words I heard that poor gal say:
"I'm goin' where my man dropped dead, Lord, Lord,
I'm goin' where my man dropped dead."

# THE JOYS OF LOVE
## (PLASIR D' AMOUR)

Starting note: Open fourth string.

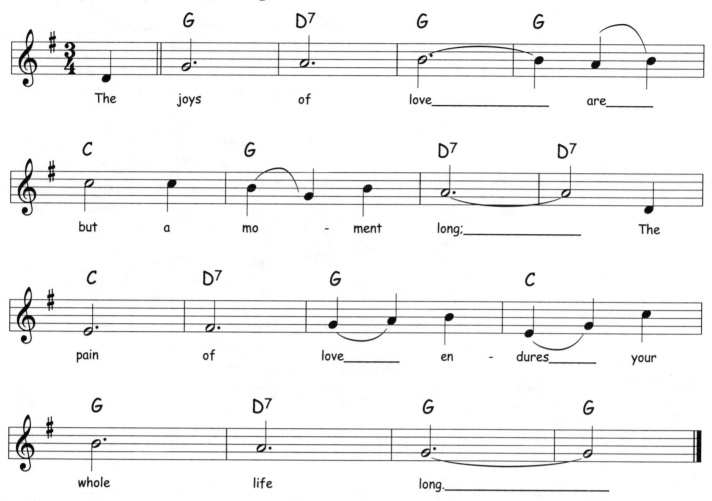

The joys of love_____ are_____
but a mo - ment long;_____ The
pain of love_____ en - dures_____ your
whole life long._____

Your eyes kissed mine,
I saw the love in them shine;
You brought me to heaven right then
When your eyes kissed mine.

And now he's gone
Like a dream that fades into dawn;
But the words stay locked in my heart strings,
My love loves me.

My love loves me,
And all the wonders I see;
A rainbow shines in my window,
My love loves me.

Plasir d'amour,
Ne dure qu' un moment;
Chagrin d'amour dure
Toute la vie.

# KINGDOM COMING

Starting note: Open fourth string.

Henry Clay Work

Say, dar - keys, hab you seen de mas-sa, Wid de muff-stash on his face, Go

long de road some time dis morn-in', Like he gwine to leab de place? He

seen a smoke, way up the rib-ber, Whar de Link-um gum-boats lay; He

took his hat, an' lef' real sud-den, An' I 'spec he's run a - way! De

**Chorus**

mas - sa run? Ha, ha! De dar - key stay? Ho, ho! It

mus' be now de king-dom com-in', An' de year ob Ju - bi - lo!

He six foot one way, two foot tudder,
An' he weigh tree hundred pound,
His coat so big, he couldn't pay the tailor,
An' it won't go half way round;
He drill so much dey call him Cap'an,
An' he get so dreffle tann'd,
I spec he try an' fool dem Yankees
For to tink he's contraband.
Chorus

De darkeys feel so lonesome libbing
In de log house on de lawn,
Dey move dar tings to massa's parlor
For to keep it while he's gone;
Dar's wine an' cider in the kitchen,
An' de darkeys dey'll hab some,
I s'pose dey'll all be cornfiscated
When de Linkum sojers come.
Chorus

De oberseer he make us trouble,
An he dribe us round a spell,
We lock him up in de smokehouse cellar,
Wid de key trown in de well;
De whip is lost, de han'cuff broken,
But de massa'll hab his pay,
He's old enough, big enough, ought to know better
Dan to went and run away.
Chorus

64

# KUM BA YA
## (COME BY HERE)

Starting note: Open third string.

Someone's singing, Lord, Kum ba ya, (3x)
Oh, Lord, Kum ba ya.

Someone's crying, Lord, Kum ba ya, (3x)
Oh, Lord, Kum ba ya.

Someone's dancing, Lord, Kum ba ya, (3x)
Oh, Lord, Kum ba ya.

Someone's praying, Lord, Kum ba ya, (3x)
Oh, Lord, Kum ba ya.

Someone's shouting, Lord, Kum ba ya, (3x)
Oh, Lord, Kum ba ya.

# LEANING ON THE EVERLASTING ARMS

Words by Rev. Elisha A. Hoffman
Music by Rev. Anthony J. Showalter

Starting note: Open second string.

What a fel-low ship, what a joy di-vine, Lean-ing on the ev-er last-ing arms; What a bless-ed-ness, what a peace is mine, Lean-ing on the ev-er-last-ing arms.

**Chorus**

Lean-ing, lean-ing, Safe and se-cure from all a-larms; Lean-ing, lean-ing, Lean-ing on the ev-er-last-ing arms.

What have I to dread, what have I to fear,
Leaning on the everlasting arms;
I have blessed peace with my Lord so near,
Leaning on the everlasting arms.
*Chorus*

O, how sweet to walk in the pilgrim's way,
Leaning on the everlasting arms;
I have blessed peace with my Lord so near,
Leaning on the everlasting arms.
*Chorus*

# LITTLE BROWN JUG

Starting note: Open fourth string.

J.E. Winner

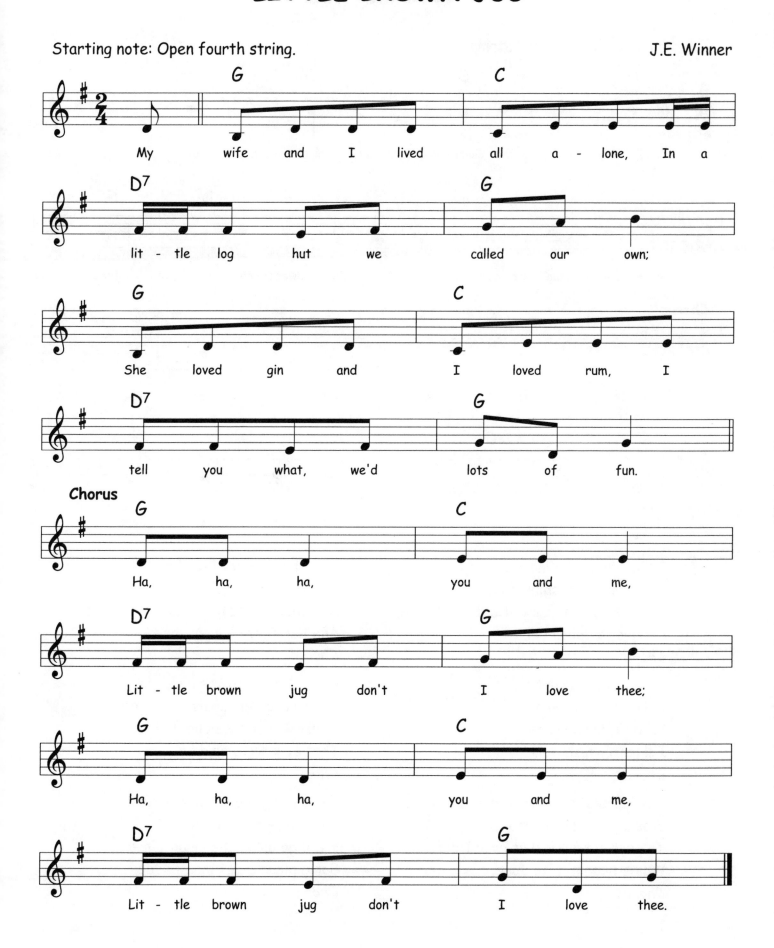

My wife and I lived all a - lone, In a
lit - tle log hut we called our own;
She loved gin and I loved rum, I
tell you what, we'd lots of fun.

**Chorus**

Ha, ha, ha, you and me,
Lit - tle brown jug don't I love thee;
Ha, ha, ha, you and me,
Lit - tle brown jug don't I love thee.

# LIZA JANE

Starting note: Open second string.

I'll go up on the moun-tain top, and plant me a batch of cane; I'll
make me a jug of mo-las-es, To sweet-en Li-za Jane.

**Chorus**

Oh, poor Li-za, li'l Li-za Jane;

Oh, poor Li-za, li'l Li-za Jane.

I'll go up on the mountain top,
Put up my moonshine still;
I'll make you a quart of old moonshine,
For just a dollar bill.
*Chorus*

When I go a-courtin',
I'll go on the train;
When I go to marry,
I'll marry Liza Jane.
*Chorus*

The hardest work that ever I did
Was a-brakin' on a train;
The easiest work that ever I did
Was a-huggin' Liza Jane.
*Chorus*

I went to see my Liza Jane,
She was standin' in the door;
Her shoes and stockings in her hand,
And her feet all over the floor.
*Chorus*

When I went to see her,
She wrung her hands and cried;
Swore I was the ugliest thing
That ever lived or died.
*Chorus*

Come along, sweet Liza Jane,
Just come along with me;
We'll go up on the mountain top,
Some pleasures there to see.
*Chorus*

# LONESOME VALLEY

Starting note: Open fourth string.

You got to walk_____ that lone - some val - ley,_____ You got to

walk_____ it for your - self;_____ Ain't no one

here_____ can walk it for you,_____ You got to

walk that lone - some val - ley by your - self._____

You must go and stand your trial,
You have to stand it by yourself;
Ain't no one else can stand it for you,
You have to stand your judgement trial by yourself.

Your mother's got to walk that lonesome valley,
She's got to walk it by herself;
Ain't no one here can walk it for her,
She's got to walk that lonesome valley by herself.

Your father's got to walk that lonesome valley . . .

Your brother's got to walk that lonesome valley . . .

Your sister's got to walk that lonesome valley . . .

God's chill'un gonna walk that lonesome valley . . .

# LONG JOURNEY HOME

Starting note: Open fourth string.

**Chorus**

Lost all my mon-ey but a two dol-lar bill,
Two dol-lar bill, Lord, two dol-lar bill;
Lost all my mon-ey but a two dol-lar bill, Now I'm
on my long jour-ney home._____

Black smoke a-rising and it looks like a train,
Looks like a train, boys, looks like a train;
Black smoke a rising and it looks like a train,
And I'm on my long journey home.
*Chorus*

It's dark and it's raining and I've got to go home,
Got to go home, boys, got to go home;
It's dark and it's raining and I've got to go home,
And I'm on my long journey home.
*Chorus*

Homesick and lonesome and I'm feeling kind of blue,
Feeling kind of blue, boys, feeling kind of blue;
Homesick and lonesome and I'm feeling kind of blue,
And I'm on my long journey home.
*Chorus*

# MAIRI'S WEDDING

Starting note: Open fourth string.

Traditional Gaelic

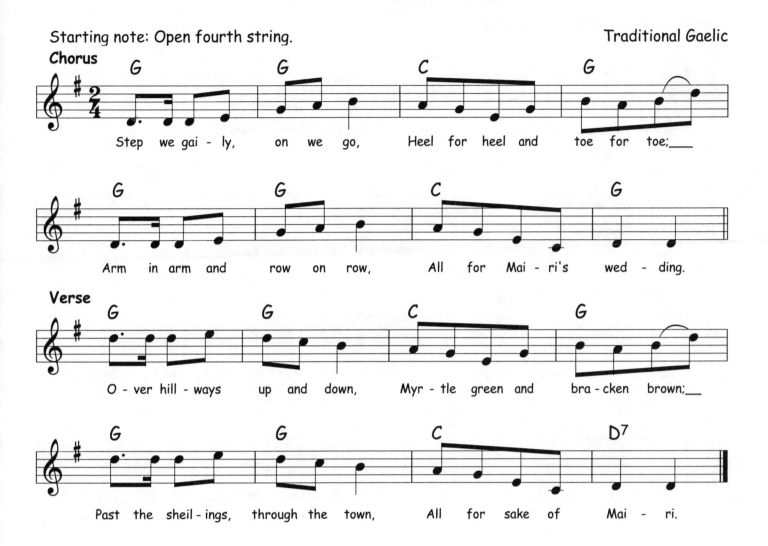

**Chorus**

Step we gai-ly, on we go, Heel for heel and toe for toe;___

Arm in arm and row on row, All for Mai-ri's wed-ding.

**Verse**

O-ver hill-ways up and down, Myr-tle green and bra-cken brown;___

Past the sheil-ings, through the town, All for sake of Mai-ri.

**Chorus**
Step we gaily, on we go,
Heel for heel and toe for toe;
Arm in arm and row on row,
All for Mairi's wedding.

Red her cheeks as rowans are,
Bright her eye as any star;
Fairest of them all by far
Is our darling Mairi.
*Chorus*

Plenty herring, plenty meal,
Plenty peat to fill her creel;
Plenty bonnie bairns as weel,
That's the toast for Mairi.
*Chorus*

*sheiling*: summer pasture on a hillside
*creel*: basket

# MAMA DON'T ALLOW

Starting note: Open third string.

Mama don't allow no banjo pickin' 'round here...

Mama don't allow no piano plunkin' 'round here...

Mama don't allow no fiddle playin' round here...

Mama don't allow no bass fiddle playin' 'round here...

Mama don't allow no Cajun music 'round here...

Etc.

Feel free to make up your own lyrics.

# MIDNIGHT SPECIAL

Starting note: Open second string.

Well, you wake up in the morn - ing, Hear the ding dong ring, You go march-in' to the ta - ble, See the same old thing; Well, now sit -tin' on the ta - ble is a fork and a pan, If you say a thing a - bout it You're in trou-ble with the man.

**Chorus**

Let the mid - night spe - cial shine it's light on me. Let the mid - night spe - cial shine it's ev - er lov -in' light on me.

If you ever go to Houston, you better walk right,
And you better not stagger, and you better not fight;
'Cause the sheriff will arrest you, and he'll carry you down,
And you can bet your bottom dollar, you're Parchman bound.
*Chorus*

Little Rosy said she loved me, but I believe she told a lie,
'Cause she hasn't been to see me since the Fourth of July;
Well, she brought a little coffee, and she brought a little tea,
Rosy gave me nearly everything but the jailhouse key.
*Chorus*

73

# NEARER, MY GOD, TO THEE

Words by Sarah Adams
Music by Lowell Mason

Starting note: Open second string.

Though like the wanderer, the sun go down,
Darkness be over me, my rest a stone;
Yet in my dreams I'd be nearer, my God, to Thee,
Nearer, my God, to Thee, nearer to Thee.

There let the way appear steps unto heaven,
All that thou sendest me in mercy given;
Angels to beckon me nearer, my God, to Thee.
Nearer, my God, to Thee, nearer to Thee.

Then with my waking thoughts bright with Thy praise,
Out of my stony griefs, Bethel I'll raise;
So by my woes to be nearer, my God, to Thee,
Nearer, my God, to Thee, nearer to Thee.

*Photo by Larry McCabe*

# NELLY BLY

Starting note: Second fret, fifth string.

Stephen Foster

Nel - ly Bly! Nel - ly Bly! Bring the broom a - long, We'll

sweep the kitch - en clean, my dear, and have a lit - tle song.

Poke the wood, my la - dy love, and make the fire____ burn. And

While I take the ban - jo down, Just give the mush a turn.

Heigh! Nel - ly, Ho! Nel - ly, lis - ten love to me, I'll

sing for you, play for you, a dul - cet mel - o - dy.

Heigh! Nel - ly, Ho! Nel - ly, lis - ten love to me, I'll

sing for you, play for you a dul - cet mel - o - dy.

Nelly Bly has a voice like a turtle dove,
I hear it in the meadow and I hear it in the grove;
Nelly Bly has a heart warm as (a) cup of tea,
And bigger than the sweet potato down in Tennessee.
*Chorus*

Nelly Bly shuts her eye when she goes to sleep,
When she wakens up again her eyeballs 'gin to peep;
The way she walks, she lifts her foot, and then she brings it down,
And when it lights there's music there in that part of the town.
*Chorus*

Nelly Bly! Nelly Bly! Never, never sigh,
Never bring the tear drop to the corner of your eye;
For the pie is made of punkins and the mush is made of corn,
And there's corn and punkins plenty, love, lyin' in the barn.
*Chorus*

# OLD FOLKS AT HOME
## (SWANEE RIVER)

OFFICIAL SONG OF THE STATE OF FLORIDA

Starting note: Open second string.

Stephen Foster

All 'round the little farm I wandered when I was young,
Then many happy days I squandered, many the songs I sung;
When I was playing with my brother, happy was I,
Oh! take me to my kind old mother, there let me live and die.
*Chorus*

# OLD MOLLY HARE

Starting note: Third fret, second string.

"Old Mol - ly hare, What -'cha do - in' there?"

"Runn - in' through the cot - ton patch as fast as I can tear."

"Old Molly hare, what'cha doin' there?"
"Sittin' at the butter dish pickin' out a hair."

"Old Molly hare, what'cha doin' there?"
"Sittin' in the haystack shootin' at a bear."

"Old Molly hare, what'cha doin there?"
"Sittin' by the fireplace smokin' my cigar."

Jump back, jump back, Molly shot a bear,
Shot him through the eye and didn't touch a hair.

# OLD TIME RELIGION

Starting note: Open fourth string.

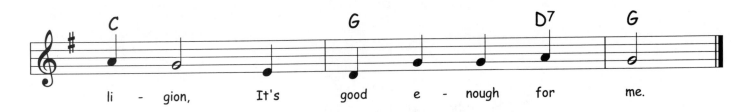

It was good enough for our fathers, (3x)
And it's good enough for me.
*Chorus*

It was good enough for our mothers, (3x)
And it's good enough for me.
*Chorus*

It was good for the Hebrew children, (3x)
And it's good enough for me.
*Chorus*

It was good for Paul and Silas, (3x)
And it's good enough for me.
*Chorus*

# OPEN UP THEM PEARLY GATES

Starting note: Second fret, fifth string.

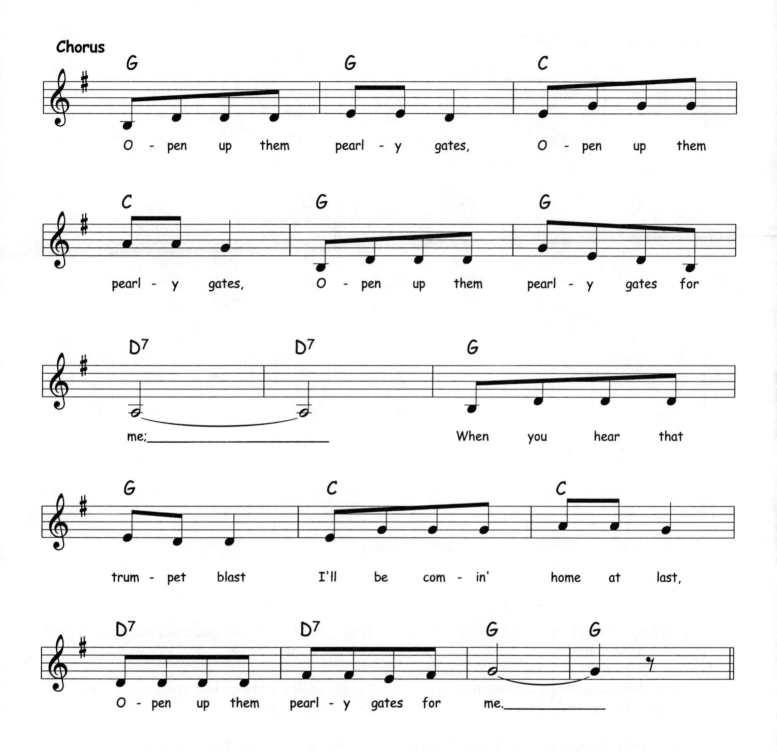

I've done had a vision,
I've seen them pearly gates a-closin',
And I seen you sinners all outside;
You better make your decision,
And pray that you'll be chosen,
Or it'll be too late when you lay down and die.
*Chorus*

You better go out to your chicken roost
And ask yourself an honest question,
And the good Lord's gonna know it if you lie;
You better turn all them chicken's loose,
Or you're gonna die from indigestion
When you eat that stolen chicken pie.
*Chorus*

# THE OTHER SHORE

Starting note: Open third string.

By and by I'll go to meet her; (3x)
On the other shore.

Won't that be a happy meeting?; (3x)
On the other shore.

There we'll shout and sing forever; (3x)
On the other shore.

There we'll meet our good old neighbors; (3x)
 On the other shore.

There we'll meet our loving mother; (3x)
On the other shore.

There we'll see our blessed Savior; (3x)
On the other shore.

# PAY ME MY MONEY DOWN

*Calypso*
Starting note: Third fret, second string.

**Chorus**

Pay me, oh, pay me,

Pay me my mon - ey down;

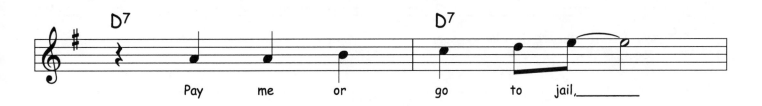

Pay me or go to jail,

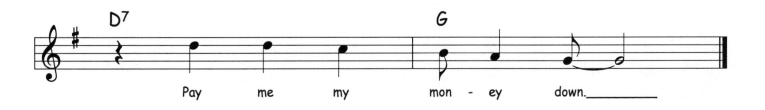

Pay me my mon - ey down.

I thought I heard the captain say,
   Pay me my money down;
Tomorrow is our sailing day,
   Pay me my money down.
Chorus

The very next day we cleared the bar,
   Pay me my money down;
He knocked me down with the end of a spar,
   Pay me my money down.
Chorus

I wish I was Mr. Howard's son,
   Pay me my money down;
Sit in the house and drink good rum,
   Pay me my money down.
Chorus

I wish I was Mr. Steven's son,
   Pay me my money down;
Sit on the bank and watch all the work done,
   Pay me my money down.
Chorus

# PRECIOUS MEMORIES

Starting note: Open fourth string.

Precious father, loving mother,
Fly across the lonely years;
And old home scenes of my childhood
In fond memory appear.
*Chorus*

As I travel on life's pathway,
Know not what the years may hold;
As I ponder, hope grows fonder,
Precious memories flood my soul.
*Chorus*

In the stillness of the midnight
Echoes from the past I hear;
Old time singing, gladness bringing
From that lovely land somewhere.
*Chorus*

# RED RIVER VALLEY

Starting note: Open fourth string.

Come and sit by my side if you love me,_____ Do not

has - ten to bid me a - dieu;_____ But re -

mem - ber the Red Riv - er Val - ley,_____ And the

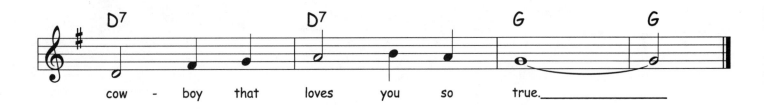

cow - boy that loves you so true._____

From this valley they say you are going,
We will miss your bright eyes and sweet smile;
For they say you are taking the sunshine
That brightens our pathway awhile.

Won't you think of the valley you're leaving?
Oh, how lonely, how sad it will be;
Oh, think of the fond heart you're breaking,
And the grief you are causing to me?

As you go to your home by the ocean,
May you never forget those sweet hours;
That we spent in the Red River Valley,
And the love we exchanged 'mid the flowers.

I have promised you, darling, that never
Will a word from my lips cause you pain;
And my life, it will be yours forever,
If you only will love me again.

# ROCK OF AGES

Words by Augustus M. Toplady
Music by Thomas Hastings

Starting note: Open fourth string.

Rock of A - ges, cleft for me, Let me
hide my - self in Thee, Let the wa - ter and the
blood from Thy wound - ed side which flowed, Be of
sin the dou - ble cure, save from wrath and make me pure.

Not the labors of my hands
Can fulfill thy law's demands,
Could my zeal no respite know,
Could my tears forever flow,
All for sin could not atone;
Thou must save, and Thou alone.

While I draw this fleeting breath,
When mine eyes shall close in death,
When I rise to worlds unknown,
And behold Thee on Thy throne,
Rock of Ages, cleft for me,
Let me hide myself in Thee.

# ROCK O' MY SOUL

Starting note: Open second string.

**Chorus**

Rock - o' my soul in the bos - om of A____ - bra - ham,

Rock - o' my soul in the bos - om of A____ - bra - ham,

Rock - o' my soul in the bos - om of A____ - bra - ham;

Oh! Rock - o' my soul!

So high, I can't get over it,
So low, I can't get under it,
So wide I can't get 'round it;
Oh! Rock o' my soul!
*Chorus*

He toted the young lambs in His bosom,
He toted the young lambs in His bosom,
He toted the young lambs in His bosom;
And left the old sheep alone.
*Chorus*

# THE ROVING GAMBLER

Starting note: Open fourth string.

I am a rov - ing gam - bler,

Gam - bled all a - round; Wher - ev - er I meet with a

deck of cards, I lay my mon - ey down.

I've gambled down in Washington,
Gambled over in Spain;
I'm on my way to Georgia
To knock down my last game.

I had not been in Washington
Many more days than three;
When I fell in love with a pretty little girl,
And she fell in love with me.

She took me in her parlor,
She cooled me with her fan;
She whispered in her mother's ear,
"I love this gambling man."

"O daughter, O dear daughter,
How could you treat me so;
To leave your dear old mother,
And with a gambler go?"

"I wouldn't marry a farmer,
For he's always in the rain;
The man I want is a gambling man
Who wears the big gold chain."

"Mother, O dear mother,
I'll tell you if I can;
If you ever see me coming back,
I'll be with the gambling man."

# RYE WHISKEY

Starting note: Open third string.

**Chorus**

I'll eat when I'm hungry,
I'll drink when I'm dry;
If the hard times don't kill me
I'll live 'til I die.

Well, its beefsteak when I'm hungry,
Hard liquor when I'm dry;
Greenbacks when I'm hard up,
And religion when I die.

Oh whiskey, oh whiskey,
You've been my downfall;
You've kicked me, you've cuffed me,
But I love you for all.

Rye whiskey, rye whiskey,
I know you of old;
You robbed my poor pockets
Of silver and gold.

Well, I used to drink bourbon,
But now I drink rye;
If the Indians don't kill me
I'll live 'til I die.

If the ocean was whiskey,
And I was a duck;
I'd dive to the bottom
And never come up.

But the ocean ain't whiskey,
And I ain't no duck;
I'll play "jack of diamonds"
And try to change my luck.

If the ocean was whiskey,
And the river was wine;
You'd find me a-fishin'
Most any old time.

Performance note: Sing the chorus after every verse or two, or as you please.

# SAINT LOUIS BLUES

Starting note: Open second string.

W.C. Handy

I hate to see_____ that eve - nin' sun go down,_____

I hate to see_____ that eve - nin' sun go down;_____

'Cause my lov - in' ma - ma has up and left this town._____

If I feel tomorrow like I feel today,
If I feel tomorrow like I feel today;
Gonna pack my trunk and make my getaway.

Been to the gypsy to get my fortune told.
Been to the gypsy to get my fortune told;
'Cause I is wild about my jelly roll.

I got the Saint Louis Blues, blue as I can be,
That gal's got a heart like a rock cast in the sea;
Or else she wouldn't gone so far from me.

I love that gal like a schoolboy loves his pie,
Like a Kentucky Colonel loves his mint and rye;
Gonna love that gal until the day I die.

You oughta see that high-struttin' gal of mine,
You oughta see that high-struttin' gal of mine;
She'd make a preacher sell his Bible, and a cross-eyed man go blind.

# SANTA LUCIA

Starting note: Open fourth string.

When o'er the waters light winds are playing,
Thy spell can sooth us, all care allaying;
To thee, sweet Napoli, what charms are given,
Where smiles creation, toil blessed by Heaven.
*Chorus*

# SILENT NIGHT

Words by Joseph Mohr
Music by Franz Gruber

Starting note: Open fourth string.

Silent Night, holy night,
Shepherds quake at the sight,
Glories stream from heaven afar,
Heavenly hosts sing Alleluia;
Christ the Savior is born!
Christ the Savior is born!

Silent Night, holy night,
Son of God, Love's pure light,
Radiant beams from Thy holy face,
With the dawn of redeeming grace;
Jesus, Lord, at Thy birth,
Jesus, Lord at Thy birth.

# SKIP TO MY LOU

Starting note: Open second string.

Chorus

Skip, skip, skip to my Lou, Skip, skip, skip to my Lou,

Skip, skip, skip to my Lou, Skip to my Lou, my dar - lin'.

Lost my part - ner, what -'ll I do? Lost my part - ner, what -'ll I do?

Lost my part - ner what -'ll I do? Skip to my Lou, my dar - lin'.

Flies in the buttermilk, shoo fly, shoo,
Flies in the buttermilk, shoo fly, shoo;
Flies in the buttermilk, shoo fly, shoo,
Skip to my lou, my darlin'.
*Chorus*

I'll get a partner better than you,
I'll get a partner better than you;
I'll get a partner better than you,
Skip to my lou, my darlin'.
*Chorus*

Can't get a red bird, a blue bird'll do,
Can't get a red bird, a blue bird'll do;
Can't get a red bird, a blue bird'll do,
Skip to my lou, my darlin'.
*Chorus*

Cat's in the cream jar, ooh ooh ooh,
Cat's in the cream jar, ooh ooh ooh;
Cat's in the cream jar, ooh ooh ooh,
Skip to my lou, my darlin'.
*Chorus*

# SOURWOOD MOUNTAIN

Starting note: Third fret, second string.

Chick - ens   a - crow - in'   on   Sour - wood   Moun - tain,

Hi,   ho,   a - doo - dle   all   day;

So   man - y   pret - ty   girls,   I   can't   count   'em,

Hi,   ho,   a - doo - dle   all   day.

I got a gal that lives in Letcher,
Hi, ho, a-doodle all day;
She ain't gonna come and I ain't gonna fetch her,
Hi, ho, a-doodle all day.

Well, the old grey goose swum the river,
Hi, ho, a-doodle all day;
If I'd have been the gander, I'd have gone with her,
Hi, ho, a-doodle all day.

My true love's a sun-burnt daisy,
Hi, ho, a-doodle all day;
She won't work and I'm too lazy,
Hi, ho, a-doodle all day.

Old man, old man, I want your daughter,
Hi, ho, a-doodle all day;
Bake my bread and carry my water,
Hi, ho, a-doodle all day.

My true love's a blue-eyed dandy,
Hi, ho, a-doodle all day;
A kiss from her is sweeter than candy,
Hi, ho, a-doodle all day.

My true love's a blue-eyed daisy,
Hi, ho, a-doodle all day;
If she won't marry me I'll go crazy,
Hi, ho, a-doodle all day.

# STAGGER LEE

Apparently based on a true story, "Stagger Lee" ("Stack Lee," "Stacker Lee," "Stagolee") shot Billy Lyons in a Memphis saloon some time before the turn of the century (1900).

Starting note: Open third string.

I was stand - ing_____ on the cor - ner,_____ When I

heard my bull - dog bark;_____ He was bark - ing at two____ men who were

gam - bling_____ in the dark.

Stagger Lee was a bad man,
Everybody knows;
Spent one hundred dollars
Just to buy one suit of clothes.

Stagger Lee and Billy Lyon
Were gamblin' late one night;
Stagger Lee threw a seven
And the two men start to fight.

"Stagger Lee," said Billy,
"I sure ain't goin' for that."
Then he showed Stack his pistol
And he stole his Stetson hat.

Next day Stagger Lee went runnin'
In the red-hot broilin' sun;
Looking for Billy
With his loaded .41.

Billy Lyon said, "Stagger Lee,
Please don't take my life;
I've got two little children
And a darling, lovely wife."

Stagger Lee shot Billy Lyon,
What do you think about that?
Shot him down like a dog
'Cause he stole his Stetson hat.

Staggger Lee, Stagger Lee,
Why don't you cut and run?
Yonder comes the policeman,
And I think he's got a gun.

There's a place in Memphis
They call the Lyon's club;
And every place that you step
You step in Billy Lyon's blood.

# STRAWBERRY ROAN

Starting note: Open third string.

I was hang - ing 'round town___ just spend - ing some time,
"Well, you fig - ured me right, I'm a good one," I claim, "Do you

Out of a job, and not mak - ing a dime; When a
hap - pen to have an - y bad ones to tame?"; He

fel - low steps up and he says, "I sup - pose that
says, "I've got one, and a bad one to buck, And a -

you're a bronc rid - er by the looks of your clothes."
throw - in' good rid - ers he's had lots of luck."

**Chorus**

Oh, that straw - ber - ry roan,_____ Oh, that

straw - ber - ry roan;_____ I'll bet all my mon - ey there's

no man a - live Who can ride old straw - ber - ry when he makes that high

dive, Stay off of that straw - ber - ry roan._____

\* The notes D-B-A-G are sometimes sung in the melody in these two measures.

100

He says, "Get your saddle, I'll give you a chance,"
So we hops in his buckboard and rides to the ranch;
In his horse corral, a-standing alone
Was this old caballero, a strawberry roan.

His legs are all spanned and he's got pigeon toes,
Little pig eyes and a big Roman nose;
Little pin ears with a split at the tip,
And a big forty-four brand upon his left hip.

He's the worst buckin' bronco I've seen on the range,
He can turn on a nickel and leave you some change;
He went up to the East, and he came down to the West,
And to stay in his middle I'm a-doin' my best.

He made one more jump, and he headed up on high,
And he left me a-sitting way up in the sky;
He made one more jump, and he came down to earth,
And I sat there cussing the day of his birth.

I know there's some ponies that I cannot ride,
There's some of them left if they haven't all died;
But I bet all my money there's no man alive
Who can ride old strawberry when he makes that high dive.

Performance note: Some cowboy singers withold the chorus, singing it only after all the verses
are sung. It is also possible to sing the chorus after every verse, or after every couple of verses.

# THE STREETS OF LAREDO

Starting note: Third fret, second string.

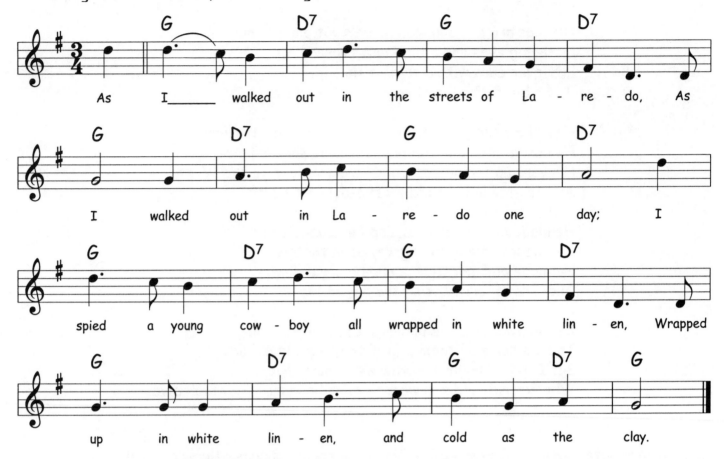

"I see by your outfit that you are a cowboy,"
These words he did say as I boldly walked by;
"Come sit down beside me and hear my sad story,
I'm shot in the breast, and I know I must die."

"It was once in the saddle I used to go dashing,
It was once in the saddle I used to go gay;
First to the cantina, and then to the gamblin',
Got shot in the breast and I'm dying today."

"Let sixteen gamblers carry my coffin,
Let sixteen cowboys sing me a song;
Take me to the graveyard and lay the sod o'er me,
For I'm a young cowboy and I know I've done wrong."

"So beat the drum slowly, play the fife lowly,
Play the death march as you carry me on;
Take me to Green Valley, lay the sod o'er me,
For I'm a young cowboy and I know I've done wrong."

# SWEET HOUR OF PRAYER

Words by Wm. W. Walford
Music by Wm. B. Bradbury

Starting note: Open third string.

Sweet hour of prayer, sweet hour of prayer,
Thy wings shall my petition bear
To Him whose truth and faithfulness
Engage the waiting soul to bless;
And since he bids me seek His face,
Believe His word and trust His grace,
I'll cast on Him my ev'ry care,
And wait for thee, sweet hour of prayer.

Sweet hour of prayer, sweet hour of prayer,
May I thy consolation share,
Till, from Mount Pisgah's lofty height,
I view my home and take my flight;
This robe of flesh I'll drop and rise
To seize the everlasting prize,
And shout, while passing thro' the air,
"Farewell, farewell, sweet hour of prayer!"

# SWING LOW, SWEET CHARIOT

Starting note: Open second string.

If you get there before I do,
Coming for to carry me home;
Tell all my friends I'm coming, too,
Coming for to carry me home.
*Chorus*

I'm sometimes up, I'm sometimes down,
Coming for to carry me home;
But still my soul feels heavenly bound,
Coming for to carry me home.
*Chorus*

# THERE IS A FOUNTAIN

Starting note: Third fret, sixth string.

William Cowper

The dying thief rejoiced to see
That fountain in his day;
And there may I, though vile as he,
Wash all my sins away:
Wash all my sins away.
Wash all my sins away;
And there may I, though vile as he,
Wash all my sins away.

Dear dying Lamb, Thy precious blood
Shall never lose its power,
Till all the ransomed church of God
Be saved, to sin no more:
Be saved, to sin no more,
Be saved to sin no more;
Till all the ransomed church of God
Be saved to sin no more.

# THIS TRAIN

Starting note: Open third string.

This train don't carry no gamblers, this train, (2x)
This train don't carry no gamblers,
No hypocrites, no midnight ramblers,
This train is bound for glory, this train.

This train don't carry no liars, this train, (2x)
This train don't carry no liars,
No hypocrites, no midnight flyers,
This train is bound for glory, this train.

This train don't carry no rustlers, this train, (2x)
This train don't carry no rustlers,
Sidestreet walkers, two-bit hustlers,
This train is bound for glory, this train.

This train is built for speed now, this train, (2x)
This train is built for speed now,
Fastest train that you ever did see,
This train is bound for glory, this train.

# TITANIC BLUES

Starting note: Third fret, second string.

Captain Smith took his glass and he walked up to the front; (2x)
He spied the iceberg a-comin' and he heard the bump.

Some was drinkin', some was playin' cards; (2x)
Some was in the corner prayin' to their God.

Children was crying: "Mama, mama what shall we do?"; (2x)
Captain Smith says, "Children, I'll take care of you."

Titanic was sinkin', sinkin' in the deep blue sea: (2x)
And the band was a-playin' "Nearer My God to Thee."

# WATERBOUND

Starting note: Open second string.

Chick - ens crow-in' in the old plough field, Chick - ens crow-in' in the old plough field;

Chick - ens crow-in' in the old plough field, Down in North Car - o - li - na.

**Chorus**

Wat - er-bound, and I can't get home, Wat - er-bound, and I can't get home;

Wat - er-bound, and I can't get home, Down in North Car - o - li - na.

Me and Tom and Dave goin' home; (3x)
Before the water rises.
*Chorus*

The old man's mad and I don't care; (3x)
Just so I get his daughter.
*Chorus*

If he don't give her up, we're gonna run away; (3x)
Down to North Carolina.
*Chorus*

I'm goin' home with the one I love; (3x)
Down to North Carolina.
*Chorus*

*Photo by Larry McCabe*

# WAY DOWNTOWN

Starting note: First fret, second string.

I wish I was over at my sweet Sally's house,
A-sittin' in that big armchair;
One arm around my old guitar,
The other around my dear.
*Chorus*

Well this good old shirt is about all I've got,
And a dollar is all I crave;
'Cause I brought nothin' with me into this old world,
Ain't gonna take nothin' to my grave.
*Chorus*

# WHAT A FRIEND WE HAVE IN JESUS

Words by Joseph Scriven
Music by Charles Converse

Starting note: Third fret, second string.

What a friend we have in Je - sus, All our sins and griefs to bear!

What a priv - i - lege to car - ry Ev - 'ry - thing to God in prayer!

O what peace we of - ten for - feit, O what need - less pain we bear,

All be - cause we do not car - ry Ev - 'ry - thing to God in prayer!

Have we trials and temptations?
Is there trouble anywhere?
We should never be discouraged,
Take it to the Lord in prayer;
Can we find a friend so faithful
Who will all our sorrows share?
Jesus knows our ev'ry weakness,
Take it to the Lord in prayer.

Are we weak and heavy laden,
Cumbered with a load of care?
Precious Savior, still our refuge,
Take it to the Lord in prayer;
Do thy friends despise, forsake thee?
Take it to the Lord in prayer,
In his arms he'll take and shield thee,
Thou wilt find a solace there.

114

# WHEN THE SAINTS GO MARCHING IN

Starting note: Open third string.

Oh, when the Saints go march-ing in, Oh, when the

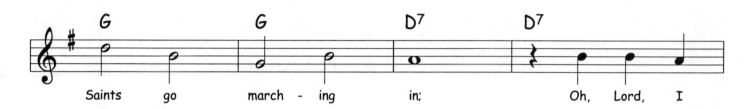

Saints go march - ing in; Oh, Lord, I

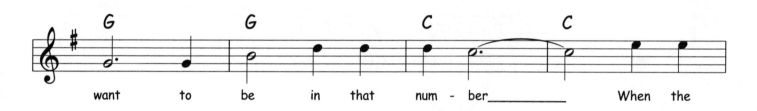

want to be in that num - ber_____ When the

Saints go march - ing in._____

Oh, when the sun refuse to shine,
Oh, when the sun refuse to shine;
Oh, Lord, I want to be in that number
When the sun refuse to shine.

When Gabriel blows that golden horn,
When Gabriel blows that golden horn;
Oh, Lord, I want to be in that number
When Gabriel blows his horn.

Oh, when they ring them silver bells,
Oh, when they ring them silver bells;
Oh, Lord, I want to be in that number
When they ring them silver bells.

And when the Revelation comes,
And when the Revelation comes;
I want to be in that number
When the Revelation comes.

# WHERE HAS MY LITTLE DOG GONE

Starting note: Open second string.

Septimus Winner

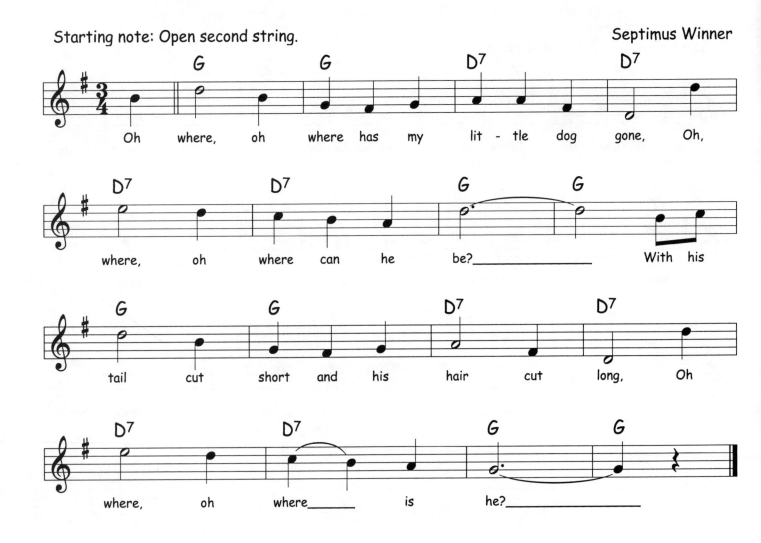

Oh where, oh where has my lit - tle dog gone, Oh,
where, oh where can he be?_____ With his
tail cut short and his hair cut long, Oh
where, oh where_____ is he?_____

I loves mine lager, 'tis very good beer,
Oh where, oh where can he be?
But with no money I cannot drink here,
Oh where, oh where is he?


Across the ocean in Germany,
Oh where, oh where can he be?
The butcher's dog is the best company,
Oh where, oh where is he?


The sausage is good, boloney of course,
Oh where, oh where can he be?
The makes them with dog and they makes them with horse,
I guess they makes them with he.

# WHERE, OH WHERE IS DEAR LITTLE SUSIE?

Starting note: Open third string.

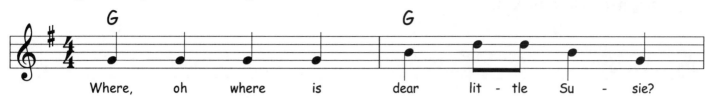

Where, oh where is dear lit - tle Su - sie?

Where, oh where is dear lit - tle Su - sie?

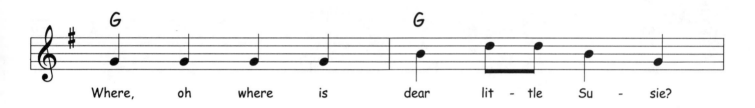

Where, oh where is dear lit - tle Su - sie?

Way down yon - der in the paw paw patch.

Come on boys, let's go find her,
Come on boys, let's go find her;
Come on boys, let's go find her,
Way down yonder in the paw paw patch.

Pickin' up paw paws, put 'em in your pocket,
Pickin' up paw paws, put 'em in your pocket;
Pickin' up paw paws, put 'em in your pocket,
Way down yonder in the paw paw patch.

# WHITE HOUSE BLUES
## (McKINLEY'S GONE)

Starting note: Open third string.

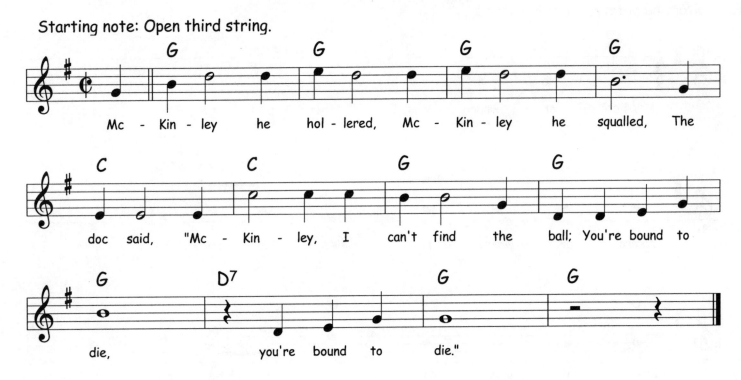

Mc - Kin - ley he hol - lered, Mc - Kin - ley he squalled, The
doc said, "Mc - Kin - ley, I can't find the ball; You're bound to
die, you're bound to die."

The doctor come a-runnin', he took off his specs,
Said, "Mr. McKinley, better cash in your checks;
You'll be gone a long, long time."

"Now hush up you children, now don't you fret,
You'll draw a pension when your pappy's dead;
I'll be gone a long long time."

"There's just one thing that grieves my mind,
That is to die and leave my poor wife behind;
I'll be gone a long, long time."

Standin' at the station, lookin' at the time,
The train's due in at half past nine;
From Buffalo to Washington.

Now yonder comes the train, she's coming down the line,
Porter tells the engineer, "McKinley's a-dyin";
It's hard times, it's hard times.

Roosevelt in the White House, drinkin' out a silver cup,
McKinley's in the graveyard, he'll never wake up;
He's gone, McKinley's gone.

# WILDWOOD FLOWER

Starting note: Open second string.

Oh, he promised to love me,
He promised to love,
To cherish me over
All others above;
I woke from my dream
And my idol was clay,
My passion for loving
Had all flown away.

I will dance and I'll sing
And my life will be gay,
I will charm every heart
In the crowd I survey;
My poor heart is wandering,
No misery can tell,
He left me no warning,
No words of farewell.

Oh, he taught me to love him,
He called me his flower,
A blossom to cheer him
Through life's dreary hour;
How I long to see him,
And regret this dark hour,
He's gone and neglected
His fair wildwood flower.

# WILL THE CIRCLE BE UNBROKEN

Starting note: Open fourth string.

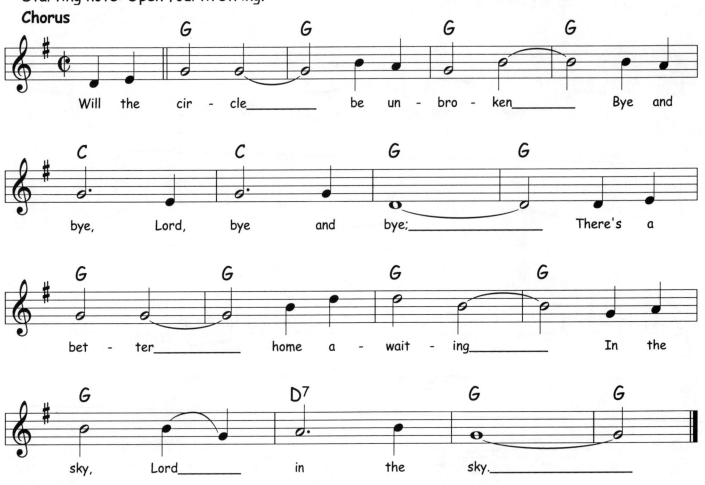

I was standing by my window
On one cold and cloudy day;
When I saw that hearse come rolling
For to carry my mother away.
*Chorus*

Lord, I told that undertaker,
"Undertaker, please drive slow;
For this body you are hauling,
Lord, I hate to see her go."
*Chorus*

I followed close behind her,
Tried to hold up and be brave;
But I could not hide my sorrow
When they laid her in the grave.
*Chorus*

# WORRIED MAN BLUES

Starting note: Open fourth string.

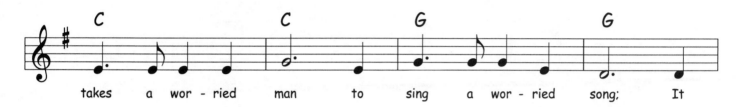

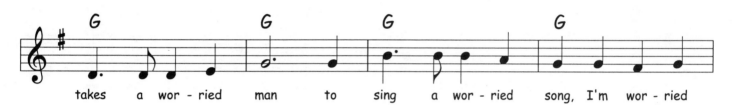

I went across the river and I laid down to sleep; (3x)
When I woke up, I had shackles on my feet.
*Chorus*

If anyone should ask you who composed this song; (3x)
Say it was I, I'll sing it all day long.
*Chorus*

Twenty-one links of chain around my leg; (3x)
And on each link is the initials of my name.
*Chorus*

I asked the judge to tell me, "What's gonna be my fine?"; (3x)
Said, "Twenty-one years on the Rocky Mountain Line."
*Chorus*

# WRECK OF THE OLD '97

Starting note: Open second string.

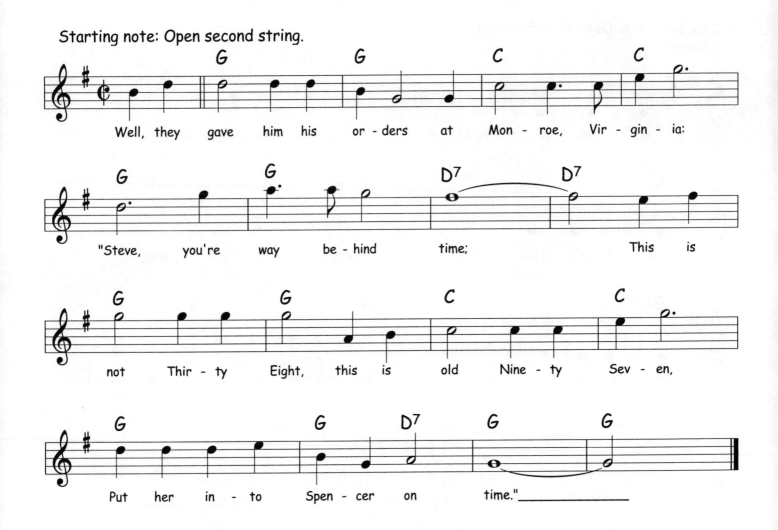

He turned and said to his big, greasy fireman:
Hey, shovel on a little more coal;
And when we cross that White Oak Mountain,
"Watch Old '97 roll!"

It's a mighty rough road from Lynchburg to Danville,
On a line on a three mile grade;
It was on that grade that he lost his airbrakes,
See what a jump he made.

He was goin' down the grade makin' ninety miles an hour,
When his whistle broke into a scream;
He was found in the wreck with his hand on the throttle,
Scalded to death by the steam.

# YANKEE DOODLE

Starting note: Open third string.

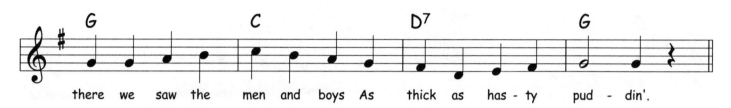

**Chorus**

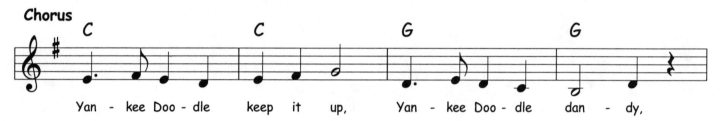

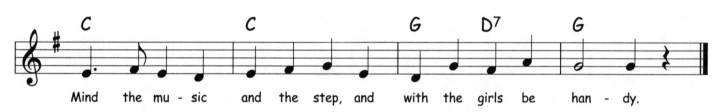

And there was Captain Washington
Upon a slapping stallion;
A-giving orders to his men,
I guess there was a million.
*Chorus*

Then I saw a swamping gun
As large as logs of maple;
Upon a very little cart
A load for father's cattle.
*Chorus*

And every time they shoot it off
It takes a horn of powder;
And makes a noise like father's gun
Only a nation louder.
*Chorus*

I saw a little barrel, too,
The head was made of leather;
They knocked upon it with some sticks
And called the folks to gather.
*Chorus*

Then they'd fife away like fun
And play on cornstalk fiddles;
And some had ribbons red as blood
All bound around their middles.
*Chorus*

Troopers, too, would gallop up
And shoot right in our faces;
It scared me almost half to death
To see them run such races.
*Chorus*

# THE YELLOW ROSE OF TEXAS

Starting note: Open fourth string.

There's a yel - low rose in Tex - as that I am going to see, No
oth - er fel - ler knows her, No - bo - dy else but me; She
cried so when I left her, it like to broke my heart, And
if I ev - er find her we will nev - er have to part.

**Chorus**
She's the sweetest little rosebud that Texas ever knew,
Her eyes are bright as diamonds, they sparkle like the dew;
You can talk about your Clementine and sing of Rosa Lee,
But the yellow rose of Texas is the only girl for me.

Where the Rio Grande is flowing, and the starry skies are bright,
She walks along the river in the quiet summer night;
She thinks if I remember, when we parted long ago,
I promised to come back again, and not to leave her so.
*Chorus*

Oh! now I'm going to find her, for my heart is full of woe,
And we'll sing the songs together, that we sung so long ago;
We'll strum the banjo gaily, and sing the songs of yore,
And the yellow rose of Texas shall be mine forever more.
*Chorus*

# OTHER MEL BAY TITLES BY LARRY McCABE

- You Can Teach Yourself™ Song Writing (MB94823BCD)

- 101 Blues Guitar Turnaround Licks (MB95360BCD)

- Famous Rock Guitar Lines (MB98430BCD)

- Famous Blues Guitar Lines (MB98428BCD)

- 101 Nashville Style Guitar Licks (MB95447BCD)

- Famous Country Guitar Lines (MB98427BCD)

- 101 Red-Hot Swing Guitar Licks (MB97335BCD)

- 101 Blues Patterns for Bass Guitar (MB95330BCD)

- 101 Amazing Jazz Bass Patterns (MB97336BCD)

- 101 Bad-to-the-Bone Blues Guitar Rhythm Patterns (MB97760BCD)

- 101 Red-Hot Bluegrass Guitar Licks and Solos (MB99445BCD)

- Famous Blues Bass Lines (MB98429BCD)